MW00323892

THE MISSING MISSING READ ME

A GUIDE FOR THE NEW SOFTWARE ENGINEER

by CHRIS RICCOMINI
and DMITRIY RYABOY

**no starch
press**

San Francisco

THE MISSING README. Copyright © 2021 by Chris Riccomini and Dmitriy Ryaboy.

All rights reserved. No part of this work may be reproduced or transmitted in any form or by any means, electronic or mechanical, including photocopying, recording, or by any information storage or retrieval system, without the prior written permission of the copyright owner and the publisher.

Printed in the United States of America

Second printing

26 25 24 23 22   2 3 4 5 6

ISBN-13: 978-1-7185-0183-6 (print)
ISBN-13: 978-1-7185-0184-3 (ebook)

Publisher: William Pollock
Production Manager: Rachel Monaghan
Production Editor: Katrina Taylor
Developmental Editor: Athabasca Witschi
Cover Design: Monica Kamsvaag
Interior Designer and Compositor: Maureen Forys, Happenstance Type-O-Rama
Copyeditor: Kim Wimpsett
Proofreader: Jamie Lauer

For information on book distributors or translations, please contact No Starch Press, Inc. directly:
No Starch Press, Inc.
245 8th Street, San Francisco, CA 94103
phone: 1-415-863-9900; info@nostarch.com
www.nostarch.com

Library of Congress Control Number: 2021938055

No Starch Press and the No Starch Press logo are registered trademarks of No Starch Press, Inc. Other product and company names mentioned herein may be the trademarks of their respective owners. Rather than use a trademark symbol with every occurrence of a trademarked name, we are using the names only in an editorial fashion and to the benefit of the trademark owner, with no intention of infringement of the trademark.

The information in this book is distributed on an "As Is" basis, without warranty. While every precaution has been taken in the preparation of this work, neither the author nor No Starch Press, Inc. shall have any liability to any person or entity with respect to any loss or damage caused or alleged to be caused directly or indirectly by the information contained in it.

[S]

PRAISE FOR *THE MISSING README*

"This is an impressively thorough overview of the many skills a new software engineer will need to learn, beyond coding, to be successful in the job. A great book for new college grads and those just entering the profession who want to see what the next phase of their career curriculum will be."

> —CAMILLE FOURNIER, former Vice President of Technology at Goldman Sachs and author of *The Manager's Path: A Guide for Tech Leaders Navigating Growth and Change*

"*The Missing README* is exactly the book I wish I had when I started my career. Fun to read, full of sage advice and priceless stories. It is like having coffee with a senior mentor, except you don't even need to come up with the right questions. Very useful for engineers early in their career, and senior engineers who wonder what they missed."

> —GWEN SHAPIRA, Engineering Leader at Confluent

"*The Missing README* is an excellent practical introduction to the day-to-day realities of software engineering in the 21st century. It covers the wide range of essential skills, techniques and heuristics that you'll need to be an effective part of any team that builds, deploys and operates production systems."

> —ADEWALE OSHINEYE, Developer Advocate at Google and co-author of *Apprenticeship Patterns*

"This book puts together all the things you don't learn on your own starting out. The information is well organized and a pleasure to read. I will be giving a copy to all my interns and new college grads."

> —THOMAS HANLEY, Senior Engineering Manager

"An accessible, handy guide to practical aspects of being a Software Engineer... The clear, README-style writing makes this book an excellent reference for any level Software Engineer from Intern to CTO."

> —TIM BURNS, Data Architect

To my family. Thanks for your love and support.

CHRIS RICCOMINI

To Gita.

DMITRIY RYABOY

About the Authors

Chris Riccomini is a software engineer with more than a decade of experience at major tech companies, including PayPal, LinkedIn, and WePay, a JP Morgan Chase Company. He has held titles as data scientist, staff software engineer, and distinguished software engineer. Riccomini is also an open source contributor and startup investor and advisor.

Dmitriy Ryaboy has been a software engineer and manager since the early 2000s. He's worked at enterprise software startups (Cloudera), consumer internet companies (Ask.com, Twitter), and research institutions (Lawrence Berkeley National Laboratory). He helped create and grow multiple open source projects, including Apache Parquet. Dmitriy is currently the vice president of software engineering at Zymergen.

BRIEF CONTENTS

CONTENTS IN DETAIL

ACKNOWLEDGMENTS

A huge thanks to our editor, Athabasca Witschi. This book wouldn't be what it is without her. Gratitude to Kim Wimpsett for copyediting help, Jamie Lauer for proofreading, and to Bill Pollock, Barbara Yien, Katrina Taylor, and others at No Starch for guiding two newbies through the book writing process.

Thanks to our review crew: Joy Gao, Alejandro Crosa, Jason Carter, Zhengliang (Zane) Zhu, and Rachel Gita Schiff. Your feedback was invaluable. Thanks to Todd Palino for feedback on operations chapters, to Matthew Clower for an honest and exhaustive review of Chapter 6, to Martin Kleppmann and Pete Skomoroch for publisher introductions and guidance, and to Tom Hanley, Johnny Kinder, and Keith Wood for feedback on the management chapters.

We couldn't have written this book without support from our employers and managers. Thanks to Chris Conrad, Bill Clerico, Aaron Kimball, and Duane Valz for letting us take a shot at this project.

PREFACE

You come into your new job ready to solve hard problems, to write elegant code, and to ply your craft. Exciting! Congratulations! We hope you get to tackle interesting challenges; work with wonderful, intelligent, and passionate colleagues; and build useful things.

But you will soon discover, or perhaps have already discovered, that knowing how to program—how to use computers to solve problems—is only half the battle. It's a critical part of your skillset, yet to be an effective software engineer, you need other skills that are not taught in school. *The Missing README* will teach you these skills.

We will explain modern practices for building, testing, and running production software, and describe behaviors and approaches that make for stronger teams and better teammates. We'll give you practical advice on how to get help, write design documents, work on old code, be on-call, plan your work, and interact with your manager and team.

This book doesn't contain everything you'll need to know—an impossible task that would make for an exhausting read. Instead, we focus on the most important information not usually covered in undergraduate computer science curricula. These topics are deep, so we end each chapter with a "Level Up" section containing recommended reading if you want more information.

The first few chapters explain what to expect when you begin your career at a company. The middle group expands your technical education: writing production-quality code, effective testing, code reviews, continuous integration and deployment, design documents, and architectural best practices. The final three chapters cover softer skills, such as Agile planning, working with your manager, and career advice.

This is an opinionated book influenced by our experiences building teams in rapidly growing, VC-funded, pre-IPO Silicon Valley companies. Your setting might be different, and that's fine. Specifics differ from company to company, but the fundamentals are universal.

The Missing README is the book we wish we had when we started out—the book we plan to give to new engineers we welcome to our teams. By the end, you'll know what it takes to be a professional software engineer. Let's get started!

THE JOURNEY AHEAD

Your journey as a software engineer spans your entire career. There are many stops along the way: student, engineer, tech lead, maybe even manager. Most new engineers start with a technical foundation but little real-world experience. The chapters ahead will guide you toward the first milestone of your career, which you'll reach when you can safely deliver code changes and work seamlessly with your team.

Reaching the first milestone is difficult—the information you need is scattered across the internet or, worse, tucked away in someone's head. This book consolidates key information that you need to be successful. But what does a successful software engineer look like, and how do you get there?

Your Destination

Everyone begins as an entry-level engineer. To advance, you'll need to be competent in several core areas.

TECHNICAL KNOWLEDGE   You know your computer science fundamentals. You know how to use integrated development environments (IDEs), build systems, debuggers, and test frameworks. You are familiar with continuous integration, metrics and monitoring, configuration, and packaging systems. You proactively create and improve test code. You consider operations when making architectural decisions.

EXECUTION   You create value by solving problems with code, and you understand the connection between your work and the business. You've built and deployed small and medium-sized features. You write, test, and review code. You share on-call duties and debug operational issues. You are proactive and dependable. You participate in technical talks, reading groups, interviews, and presentations.

COMMUNICATION   You communicate clearly both in written and verbal form. You are able to give and receive feedback effectively. You proactively ask for help and get clarification in ambiguous situations. You raise issues and identify problems in a constructive manner. You provide help when possible and are starting to influence peers. You document your work. You write clear design documents and invite feedback. You are patient and empathetic when dealing with others.

LEADERSHIP   You work independently on well-scoped work. You learn from mistakes quickly. You handle change and ambiguity well. You actively participate in project and quarterly planning. You help new team members onboard. You give meaningful feedback to your manager.

A Map for Your Journey

To get to your destination, you need a map. The rest of this chapter will help you navigate both this book and the beginning of your career. We start at Peak Newb, where all newbies begin. From there, we travel down Ramp-Up River, where you start coding and learning local conventions and processes. Next is Cape Contributor, where you ship some meaningful features. Shipping features means you will have to sail the storms of Operations Ocean. Finally, we will land in the safe haven of Competence Cove.

We've annotated many paragraphs with chapter references. You can read this book linearly, or you can jump to the chapters you care most about. Many chapter references appear more than once in the outline; this is intentional. Chapters are grouped by subject, but the subjects we cover will span your career. You will discover new insights every time you revisit the material.

Peak Newb

You begin your journey as a newbie. Get familiar with the company, the team, and how things get done. Attend onboarding meetings. Set up your development environment and system access, and figure out regular team processes and meetings. Read documentation and have discussions with teammates. Contribute by filling in documentation gaps you find in the onboarding process.

Your company might have a new hire orientation to help you get up and running. These programs teach you how the company works, provide a tour of the organization, and introduce company leadership. New hire programs also introduce you to new hires from other departments—your future colleagues. If your company doesn't have a new hire program, ask your manager to explain the "org chart" (who is in charge of what and who reports to whom), the different departments, and how they relate; take notes.

CUNNINGHAM'S LAW AND BIKE-SHEDDING

We advise you to document conventions, onboarding procedures, and other oral traditions on your team. You will get a lot of comments and corrections. Do not take the comments personally. The point is not to write a perfect document but rather to write enough to trigger a discussion that fleshes out the details. This is a variation of *Cunningham's law*, which states that "the best way to get the right answer on the internet is not to ask a question; it's to post the wrong answer."

Be prepared for trivial discussions to become drawn out, a phenomenon called *bike-shedding*. Bike-shedding is an allegory by C. Northcote Parkinson, describing a committee assigned to review designs for a power plant. The committee approves the plans within minutes, as they are too complex to actually discuss. They then spend 45 minutes discussing the materials for the bike shed next to the plant. Bike-shedding comes up a lot in technical work.

Some companies have additional new software engineer onboarding processes to help you get access to systems, set up your development environment, and check out and build code. If no such process exists, you have an opportunity to create one! Write down what you do as you set up. (See Chapter 2, "Getting to Conscious Competence.")

You should get assigned a small task to learn the basics of making a code change and shepherding it into production. If not, look or ask for some useful—but minor—change to make. It can be as small as updating a comment; the goal is to understand the steps, not to impress. (See Chapter 2, "Getting to Conscious Competence," and Chapter 8, "Delivering Software.")

Set up your code editor or IDE. Use the IDE that your team uses; if you don't know it, find a tutorial online. Learning your IDE will save you a lot of time later. Configure your IDE to apply team code formatting conventions; ask what they are and how to apply them. (See Chapter 3, "Working with Code.")

Make sure your manager adds you to team and company meetings—stand-ups, sprint planning, retrospectives, all-hands, and so on. Remind your manager to schedule a one-on-one meeting if they conduct them. (See Chapter 12, "Agile Planning," and Chapter 13, "Working with Managers.")

Ramp-Up River

Once you've completed newbie tasks, you'll take on your first real work for the team. You will probably work on an existing codebase. What you find might confuse or intimidate you. Ask questions, and have your team review your work frequently. (See Chapter 3, "Working with Code," and Chapter 7, "Code Reviews.")

Learning is critical as you ramp up. Investigate how code is built, tested, and deployed. Read pull requests and code reviews. Don't be afraid to ask for more information. Sign up for tech talks, brown bags, reading groups, mentorship programs, and the like. (See Chapter 2, "Getting to Conscious Competence"; Chapter 5, "Managing Dependencies"; Chapter 6, "Testing"; and Chapter 8, "Delivering Software.")

Now is the time to build a relationship with your manager. Get to know their working style, understand their expectations, and talk to them about your goals. If your manager does one-on-ones, expect to have your first few sessions. Managers usually want to track progress, so ask your manager how to communicate status. (See Chapter 13, "Working with Managers.")

You'll probably also attend your first planning session, usually a sprint planning meeting. You might also join retrospective or all-hands meetings. Ask for an overview of the roadmap and development planning process. (See Chapter 12, "Agile Planning.")

Cape Contributor

You'll enter Cape Contributor once you begin working on larger tasks and features. The team trusts you to work more independently. Learn how to write production-grade code that's operator friendly, properly manages dependencies, and has clean tests. (See Chapter 3, "Working with Code"; Chapter 4, "Writing Operable Code"; Chapter 5, "Managing Dependencies"; and Chapter 6, "Testing.")

You should be helping teammates now, too. Get involved in code reviews, and expect teammates to ask for ideas and feedback. Your team might forget that you've joined recently, so ask questions when you're confused. (See Chapter 2, "Getting to Conscious Competence"; Chapter 7, "Code Reviews"; and Chapter 10, "Technical Design Process.")

Most companies have quarterly planning and goal-setting cycles. Participate in team planning, and work with your manager to set goals or objectives and key results (OKRs). (See Chapter 12, "Agile Planning," and Chapter 13, "Working with Managers.")

Operations Ocean

You'll learn more about how code is delivered to users as you work on larger tasks. A lot happens during delivery: testing, build, release, deployment, and rollout. Finessing this process takes skill. (See Chapter 8, "Delivering Software.")

After rolling out your changes, you'll have to operate your team's software. Operations work is high stress and takes grit; customers will be impacted by instability. You'll debug live software using metrics, logs, and trace tools. You might also enter an on-call rotation at this point. Exposure to operational work will show you how code behaves in users' hands, and you'll learn to protect your software. (See Chapter 4, "Writing Operable Code," and Chapter 9, "Going On-Call.")

Competence Cove

Your team will count on you to drive a small project now. You'll need to write a technical design document and help with project planning. Designing software will expose you to a new level of complexity. Don't settle for your first design; explore trade-offs and plan for your system to evolve over time. (See Chapter 10, "Technical Design Process"; Chapter 11, "Creating Evolvable Architectures"; and Chapter 12, "Agile Planning.")

Some of the early shine of your job has worn off. You see flaws in the architecture, the build and deploy system, and the testing environment. You are learning to balance regular work with necessary maintenance and refactoring. Don't try to rewrite everything. (See Chapter 3, "Working with Code.")

You also have thoughts about team processes. Write down your observations—what's working and what isn't—and discuss your ideas in a one-on-one with your manager. (See Chapter 13, "Working with Managers.")

Now is also the time to work on longer-term goal setting and performance reviews. Work with your manager to understand the process and get feedback from peers. Discuss career aspirations, future work, projects, and ideas with your manager. (See Chapter 13, "Working with Managers," and Chapter 14, "Navigating Your Career.")

Onward!

You now have both a map and destination for your beginner's journey. After landing at Competence Cove, you'll be a full-fledged software engineer capable of working with your team to deliver valuable features. The remainder of the book will help you navigate the path. Our journey begins.

GETTING TO CONSCIOUS COMPETENCE

Martin M. Broadwell defines four stages of competence in *Teaching for Learning*: unconscious incompetence, conscious incompetence, conscious competence, and unconscious competence. Specifically, *unconscious incompetence* means you are unable to perform a task correctly and are unaware of the gap. *Conscious incompetence* means you are unable to perform a task correctly but are aware of the gap. *Conscious competence* means you are capable of performing a task with effort. Finally, *unconscious competence* means you are capable of performing a task effortlessly.

All engineers start out consciously or unconsciously incompetent. Even if you know everything about software engineering (an impossible task), you're going to have to learn company-specific processes and rules. You're also going to have to learn practical skills like those covered in this book. Your goal is to get to conscious competence as quickly as possible.

The bulk of this chapter discusses learning on your own and getting help. Learning outside of school is a skill; we offer some suggestions for developing an independent learning habit. We also provide tips for balancing between asking for help too much and not enough. The chapter finishes by discussing impostor syndrome and the Dunning–Kruger effect, which can cause new engineers to feel under- or overconfident and limit their growth. We explain how to detect and combat both of these extremes. Practicing independent learning and asking effective questions while avoiding traps of self-doubt and overconfidence will get you to conscious competence quickly.

Learning to Learn

Learning will help you become a competent engineer and flourish in the years to come. The field of software engineering is constantly evolving; whether you are a new grad or a seasoned veteran, if you're not learning, you're falling behind.

This section is a digest of various approaches to learning. Don't try to do everything that's listed in this chapter at the same time! That's a recipe for burnout. Guard your personal time—continued growth is important, but spending every waking moment on work is unhealthy. Choose from the list based on your circumstances and natural inclinations.

Front-Load Your Learning

Spend your first few months on the job learning how everything works. This will help you participate in design discussions, on-call rotations, operational issues, and code reviews. Front-loaded learning will be uncomfortable—you'll want to ship software, and taking time to read documentation and fiddle with tools will slow you down. Don't worry; everyone expects you to spend time ramping up. Front-loaded learning is an investment, one that is so valuable that many companies explicitly design a learning curriculum for new hires. Facebook, famously, has a six-week "boot camp" for new engineers.

Learn by Doing

Front-loaded learning does not mean sitting around reading documentation all day. We learn a little by reading and a lot by doing. You should write and ship code. Shipping code for the first time is scary—what if you break something?—but managers won't usually put you in a situation where you can do serious damage (though sometimes new hires do high-risk work when there's no alternative). Do your best to understand the impact of your work, and act with an appropriate level of caution. You can be less cautious, and thus faster, writing a unit test than you can be altering indexes on a high-traffic database.

THE DAY CHRIS DELETED ALL OF THE CODE

At one of Chris's first internships, he was working on a project with a senior engineer. Chris finished some changes and needed to get them deployed. The senior engineer showed him how to check code into the revision control system, CVS. Chris followed the instructions, blindly running through steps that involved branching, tagging, and merging. Afterward, he continued with the rest of his day and went home. The next morning, Chris strolled in cheerfully and greeted everyone. They did their best to respond in kind, but they were low. When Chris asked what was up, they informed him that he had managed to corrupt the entire CVS repository. All of the company's code had been lost. They had been up the entire night desperately trying to recover what they could and were eventually able to get most of the code back (except for Chris's commits and a few others). Chris was pretty shaken by the whole thing. His manager pulled him aside and told him not to worry: Chris had done the right thing working with the senior engineer. Mistakes happen. Every engineer has some version of a story like this. Do your best, and try to understand what you're doing, but know that these things happen.

Mistakes are unavoidable. Being a software engineer is hard, and we're all expected to fail sometimes. Everyone knows and expects this. It's your manager's and team's job to maintain safety nets to make these failures nonfatal. If and when you fail, don't beat yourself up: write down lessons learned, and move on.

Experiment with Code

Run experiments to learn how code truly works. Documentation goes out-of-date. Coworkers forget things. Experiments are safe since you can run them outside of production, and nonproduction experiments allow for more invasive techniques. For example, you might know that a method is invoked but be unable to determine how it's reached. Experiment by throwing an exception, printing a stack trace, or attaching a debugger to see the call path.

Debuggers are your best friend when experimenting. You can use them to pause running code and see running threads, stack traces, and variable values. Attach a debugger, trigger an event, and step through the code to see how the code processes the event.

Although debuggers are powerful, sometimes the easiest way to understand a behavior is a few well-placed log lines or print statements. You are probably familiar with this method; just be aware that in complex scenarios, particularly with multithreaded applications, print debugging may be misleading. Operating systems will buffer writes to standard output, delaying what you see in the console, and multiple threads writing to standard output will interleave their messages.

One silly but surprisingly useful technique is to add a distinctive print statement at the beginning of the program's execution so you can easily tell if you are running your modified program instead of the original. You'll save yourself hours of chasing mysterious behaviors that come down to the unmodified program being invoked instead of the one you are changing.

Read

Spend a portion of each week reading. There are many different sources: team documentation, design documents, code, ticket backlogs, books, papers, and technical sites. Don't try to read everything all at once. Start with team documentation and design documents. These will give you a broad overview of how things fit together. Pay special attention to discussions on trade-offs and context. You can then take a deep dive into subsystems that are relevant to your first few tasks.

As Ron Jeffries says, "Code never lies. Comments sometimes do" (*https:// ronjeffries.com/articles/020-invaders-70ff/i-77/*). Read code—it doesn't always match the design document! Not just your codebase: read high-quality open source code, particularly libraries you use. Don't read code front to back like a novel: use your IDE to navigate through the codebase. Diagram control flow and states for key operations. Dig into the code's data structures and algorithms. Pay attention to edge case handling. Keep an eye out for idioms and style—learn the "local dialect."

Pending work is tracked in *tickets* or *issues*. Read through team tickets to see what everyone is working on and what is coming up. The backlog is a good place to find newbie tickets, too. Old tickets fall into three broad categories: no longer relevant, useful but minor, and important but too large to tackle at the moment. Figure out which of these categories the tickets you are looking at fall into.

Published and online resources complement each other. Books and papers are great for going deep into a subject. They are reliable but more dated. Online resources such as Twitter, blogs, and newsletters are the opposite: less trustworthy but great for keeping up with trends. Just remember to pump the brakes before implementing the latest ideas from Hacker News: it's good to be boring (more on this in Chapter 3).

Join a reading group to keep up with research in academia and industry. Some companies have internal reading groups—ask around. If your company does not, consider starting one. You can also join a local Papers We Love chapter; these groups read and discuss computer science papers regularly.

LEARNING TO READ CODE

Early in his career, Dmitriy was handed a legacy Java application and asked to "figure it out." He was the only person on the team who was even moderately comfortable with Java, and his manager wanted to make some changes. The source code was full of . . . peculiarities. All the variables had names like a, b, and c. To make things worse, an a in one function would be a d in another. There was no source control history, no tests. The original developer had long since left. Needless to say, it was a minefield.

Every time Dmitriy needed to change anything in the codebase, he blocked out all the distractions and carefully read the code, renamed variables, traced the logic, sketched things on paper, experimented. It was slow going. Dmitriy grew to appreciate the codebase. It was doing complex things. He was a little in awe of whoever wrote this thing: to keep all this in their head without sensible variable names! Eventually, over lunch Dmitriy expressed this tempered admiration. His colleague looked at him as if he'd grown a second head. "Dmitriy, we don't have the original source code. You are working on the output of a decompiler. No one in their right mind would write code that way!" We don't recommend this as a way to learn to read code; but, boy, did that experience teach Dmitriy to go slowly, read for comprehension, and never trust variable names.

Watch Presentations

You can learn a lot from a good presentation. Start with recorded video presentations from the past—both internal company talks and external YouTube videos. Watch tutorials, tech talks, and conference presentations. Ask around to find good content. You can usually watch videos at 1.5 or even 2x speed to save time, but do not watch passively. Take notes to help with retention, and follow up on any unfamiliar concepts or terms.

Go to *brown bags* and tech talks if your company offers them. These informal presentations are hosted on-site, so they're easy to get to. They're also internal to your company, so you'll get really relevant information.

Attend Meetups and Conferences (Sparingly)

Conferences and meetups are good for networking and discovering new ideas. They are worth attending occasionally, but don't overdo it. The signal-to-noise ratio—the ratio of relevant content to all content—is often low, and many presentations are available online afterward.

There are roughly three types of conferences: academic conferences, grassroots interest group gatherings, and vendor showcases. Academic conferences have great content, but reading papers and going to smaller, more focused get-togethers is usually better. Interest-based conferences are great for getting practical tips and meeting experienced practitioners; check out a few. Vendor conferences are the biggest and most visible. They are marketing vehicles for large tech companies and not great for learning. They are fun to attend with your coworkers, but more than one per year is likely a waste of time. Ask around to find the best ones. Keep in mind that some employers will pay for the tickets, travel, and lodging.

CRASHING THE ACADEMIC PARTY

Years ago, Dmitriy and his colleague Peter Alvaro were struggling to make their data warehouse perform and thought distributing the aggregation tasks to a cluster of commodity servers was the way to go. During their research, Peter found Google's recently released MapReduce paper. The mighty Google was doing what Peter and Dmitriy were proposing! They found more interesting papers and wanted to find people to talk to about them. Dmitriy discovered that the UC Berkeley database group hosted lunches that were technically open to the public. Peter and Dmitriy became regulars (they

(continued)

were careful not to eat the free pizza until all the students had their fill). They could even occasionally contribute to the conversation!

Their learning shifted into high gear. Eventually, Peter stayed for good—he enrolled in the Berkeley PhD program and is now a professor at UC Santa Cruz. Dmitriy, too, jumped to grad school. The expensive data warehouse was replaced by Hadoop, an open source distributed aggregation system, two years after they left.

If you start feeling that you are no longer learning, check the local university. They have a ton of programs that are open to the public. Expand your circle and get exposed to new ideas. Going to grad school is optional.

Shadow and Pair with Experienced Engineers

Shadowing is following another person as they perform a task. The shadower is an active participant: they take notes and ask questions. Shadowing a senior engineer is a great way to learn a new skill. To get the most out of it, set up time before and after the shadowing session for planning and retrospection.

Reverse roles when you are ready. Have a senior engineer shadow you. Like you, they should provide feedback. They will also act as a safety net if things go wrong. This is a gentle way to ease into scary situations like interviewing.

Pair programming is also a great way to learn. Two engineers write code together, taking turns doing the typing. It takes some getting used to, but it's one of the fastest ways to learn from each other. Advocates of this technique also claim that it raises code quality. If your teammates are willing, we highly recommend trying it. Pair programming isn't just for junior engineers, either. Teammates of all levels can benefit from it.

Some companies also encourage shadowing nonengineering roles. Shadowing customer support and sales demos is an eye-opening way to learn about your customers. Write down and share your observations.

Work with your manager and senior engineers to prioritize ideas inspired by the experience.

Experiment with Side Projects

Working on side projects will expose you to new technologies and ideas. You can skip the "software engineering stuff" (testing, operations, code reviews, and so on) when you're working on your own. Ignoring these aspects lets you learn new technologies quickly; just don't forget about the "real" stuff at work.

You can also participate in open source projects. Most projects welcome contributions. This is a great way to learn and build professional connections. You might even find future jobs through open source communities. Keep in mind that these projects are often run by volunteers. Don't expect the same turnaround speed you get at work. Sometimes people will get busy and disappear for a bit.

Don't choose a project based on what you think you need to learn. Find problems you are interested in solving, and solve those problems using the tools you want to learn. A goal that intrinsically motivates you will keep you engaged longer, and you'll learn more.

Companies have rules about outside work. Ask for your company's policy. Don't use company resources (your company laptop) to work on side projects. Don't work on side projects at work. Avoid side projects that compete with your company. Clarify whether you can contribute to open source at work or at home. Some companies will want you to contribute only under special work accounts. Others will want you to use personal accounts only. Understand whether you retain ownership over your side projects. Ask your manager if you need to get approvals. Getting clarity will save you frustration in the long run.

Asking Questions

All engineers should ask questions—it's a critical part of learning. New engineers worry about bothering teammates and try to figure everything out themselves instead. This is slow and inefficient. Asking questions effectively will help you learn quickly without irritating others. Use these three steps: do research, ask clear questions, and time your questions appropriately.

Do Your Research

Try to find the answer yourself. Even if your colleagues know the answer, put in the effort—you'll learn more. If you don't find the answer, your research will still be your starting point when you ask for help.

Don't just search the internet. Information lives in documentation, wikis, READMEs, source code, and bug trackers. If your question is about code, try turning it into a unit test that demonstrates the problem. It's possible your question has been asked before: check the mailing list or chat group archives. The information you gather will lead to ideas that you can test. If you can't find any leads, try to work it out yourself by experimenting. Keep track of where you looked, what you did, why you did it, what happened, and what you learned.

Timebox

Limit how long you research a question. Set the limit before you start your research to encourage discipline and prevent diminishing returns (research will eventually stop being productive). Consider when you need to know the answer, and then leave enough time to ask a question, get an answer, and act on what you learn.

Once you reach the end of your timebox, ask for help. Only exceed the timebox if you are making good progress. If you go past your first time-box, set another. If you are still not sure of the answer after the second timebox, cut your losses and ask for help. Stopping takes discipline and practice—hold yourself accountable.

Show Your Work

Describe what you know when asking a question. Don't just share your raw notes. Outline what you've tried and discovered succinctly. This signals that you have spent time trying to figure out the problem yourself. It also gives others a starting point for their answer.

This is a poor way to ask a question:

Hey Alice,

Any idea why testKeyValues is failing in TestKVStore? It really slows down our builds to rerun this.

Thanks!

Pankaj

This gives Alice little to go on. It sounds vaguely like Pankaj is blaming Alice for something, which is probably not what he intended. It's a little lazy. Compare this with the following:

Hey Alice,

I'm having trouble figuring out why testKeyValues is failing in TestKVStore (in the DistKV repo). Shaun pointed me your way. I'm hoping you can help.

The test fails for me about every third execution; it seems random. I tried running it in isolation, and it's still failing, so I don't think it's an interaction between tests. Shaun ran the test in a loop on his machine but was unable to reproduce it. I don't see anything obvious in the source code to explain the failure. It seems like some kind of race condition. Any thoughts?

There is no terrible urgency around this as I'm told this is unlikely to be affecting production. Still, the flapping test costs us 20–30 minutes every time this happens, so I'd love to figure out how to fix it. I've attached logs that show failures and all of my current environment settings, just in case.

Thanks!

Pankaj

In the second example, Pankaj gives some context, describes the problem, tells Alice what he's already tried, and asks for help. He also notes both the impact and the level of urgency. It is succinct but has detailed information attached so Alice doesn't need to hunt for it. Alice will help Pankaj out. She will also remember that Pankaj is thorough. Requests like this will build Pankaj's credibility in the eyes of his colleagues.

It takes more effort to write the second message. It's worth it. Put in the work.

Don't Interrupt

Just like you, others are trying to get things done; they need to focus. When they're in the zone, don't interrupt them. Even if the question is easy. Even if you know they know the answer. Even if you're blocked. Unless there is a critical issue, really, don't interrupt them.

Companies have different conventions to signal "Don't interrupt." Headphones, ear plugs, or earmuffs are universal. There's some confusion about "lounge spaces." Some consider working somewhere other than their desk sacrosanct—they don't want to be found. Others interpret engineers in shared spaces as "available to interrupt." Make sure you understand your company's convention!

Walking up and talking to someone forces them to respond. Even if they just reply that they're busy, you've already interrupted and caused them to lose focus. You're not stuck if the person you need is busy. You need to find an asynchronous way to communicate.

Prefer Multicast, Asynchronous Communication

In networking, *multicasting* means sending a message to a group instead of an individual destination. *Asynchronous* means a message that can be processed later, rather than requiring an immediate response. These concepts apply to human communication, too.

Post questions so that multiple people can respond (multicast) at their own pace (asynchronous). Do this in a way that's visible to everyone so it's apparent when you've been helped. The answer will also be discoverable, so others can find the discussion later.

This usually means using a group mailing list or group chat (for example, Dmitriy's company has a #sw-helping-sw channel). Use shared forums even if you need an answer from a specific person; you can mention their name in your post.

Batch Your Synchronous Requests

Chat and email are great for simple questions, but complex discussions don't work asynchronously. In-person conversations are "high bandwidth" and "low latency." You can cover a lot quickly. This is costly, though. Interrupting your coworkers affects their productivity. Avoid this by setting up dedicated time with your tech lead or manager for nonurgent questions. Schedule a meeting, or use "office hours" if they exist. Write down questions and hold them until the meeting. You can do your research in the meantime. Your list will grow as other questions arise. This is good. Include the list in your meeting agenda. Don't rely on your memory, and don't come unprepared.

Cancel the meeting if you have no questions. If you find yourself canceling repeatedly, ask whether the meeting is still useful—if not, unschedule it.

Overcoming Growth Obstacles

Knowing how to learn and ask questions isn't enough. You must also avoid traps that slow growth. Two common impediments, impostor syndrome and the Dunning–Kruger effect, affect many engineers. You will grow faster if you understand what these phenomena are and how to overcome them.

Impostor Syndrome

Most new engineers start off consciously incompetent. There's a lot to learn, and everyone else seems far ahead. You might worry that you don't belong or that landing your job was luck. It's easy to be hard on yourself—we've experienced this ourselves. No matter how often we tell engineers they're doing a great job, some don't believe it, even when they're getting promoted! It makes them uncomfortable. They say they've gotten lucky, they don't deserve recognition, or the promotion criteria are too lax. This is *impostor syndrome*. It was first described in a 1978 study by Drs. Pauline Rose Clance and Suzanne Ament Imes, "The Impostor Phenomenon in High Achieving Women: Dynamics and Therapeutic Intervention."

> *Despite outstanding academic and professional accomplishments, women who experience the impostor phenomenon persist in believing that they are really not bright and have fooled anyone who thinks otherwise. Numerous achievements, which one might expect to provide ample objective evidence of superior intellectual functioning, do not appear to affect the impostor belief.*

If this resonates with you, know that self-doubt is common. With effort, these feelings will pass. You can move things along with several strategies: awareness, reframing, and talking to colleagues.

Impostor syndrome is self-reinforcing. Every error is seen as proof of incompetence, while every success is evidence of a good "faker." Once an individual enters this cycle, it is difficult to get out of. Awareness helps: if you watch for this pattern, you can consciously break it. When you accomplish something, it's because you actually did it—you aren't just getting lucky.

Don't dismiss compliments and accomplishments. Write them down, even the small stuff. Your peers are capable, and if they say something positive, they have good reason to. Practice reframing negative thoughts: "I had to bug Daria to help with a race condition" becomes "I reached out to Daria, and now I know how to resolve race conditions!" Plan what you want to accomplish and notice when you achieve a goal. This will build confidence.

Getting feedback also helps. Ask someone you respect to tell you how you're doing. This can be your manager, a mentor, or just an engineer you look up to. The important thing is that you trust them and feel safe talking to them about self-doubt.

Therapy might also help. Use it to gain comfort with your strengths and work through short-term challenges. Impostor syndrome, and the anxiety and depression that can accompany it, is a complex topic. If you are struggling, consider talking to a few therapists to find one whose approach works for you.

The Dunning–Kruger Effect

Opposite to impostor syndrome is the *Dunning–Kruger effect*, a cognitive bias where people believe that they're more capable than they actually are. Unconsciously incompetent engineers don't know what they don't know, so they can't accurately evaluate their performance (or anyone else's). They are too confident; they storm around critiquing the company's technical stack, complaining about code quality, and belittling design. They are certain that their ideas are right. Their default mode is to push back on or disregard feedback. Rejecting all suggestions serves as a giant red light: complete confidence is the sign of a blind spot.

Fortunately, the Dunning–Kruger effect is less common among new engineers. There are many ways to fight it. Start by consciously developing curiosity. Be open to being wrong. Find a respected engineer, ask how you're doing, and truly listen. Talk over design decisions, especially those you don't agree with. Ask why the decisions were made. Cultivate a mindset of trade-offs, not of right and wrong.

Do's and Don'ts

DO'S	DON'TS
DO play and experiment with code.	**DON'T** just churn out code.
DO read design documents and other people's code.	**DON'T** be afraid to take risks and fail.
DO join meetups, online communities, interest groups, and mentorship programs.	**DON'T** overdo conferences.
DO read papers and blogs.	**DON'T** be afraid to ask questions.
DO prefer multicast and asynchronous communication.	
DO shadow interviews and on-call rotations.	

Level Up

Dave Hoover and Adewale Oshineye's *Apprenticeship Patterns: Guidance for the Aspiring Software Craftsman* (O'Reilly Media, 2009) is a great collection of "patterns" one can use to get started in a new environment, seek guidance, learn skills deeply, and overcome common hurdles.

For more on asking questions, we recommend *All You Have to Do Is Ask: How to Master the Most Important Skill for Success* by Wayne Baker (Currency, 2020). This book is divided into two parts. The first section discusses the value of asking questions and why it's hard. The second half of the book is a toolkit for asking questions effectively.

For more on pair programming, the classic text is *Extreme Programming Explained: Embrace Change* by Kent Beck and Cynthia Andres (Addison-Wesley, 2004). The book covers much more than just pair programming. If you are interested in a shorter read, the article "On

Pair Programming" by Birgitta Böckeler and Nina Siessegger at *https://www.martinfowler.com/articles/on-pair-programming.html* is an excellent practical guide.

If you find that the impostor syndrome or Dunning–Kruger sections resonate, check out *Presence: Bringing Your Boldest Self to Your Biggest Challenges* by Amy Cuddy (Little, Brown & Company, 2016). Many common causes of both work anxiety and overconfidence are covered in the book.

WORKING WITH CODE

There's an ancient Roman amphitheater in Arles, France. It used to provide entertainment—chariot races and gladiatorial combat—for up to 20,000 people. After the fall of Rome, a small town was built right in the arena. This made sense; it had walls and a drainage system. Later inhabitants probably found the setup odd and inconvenient. They might have judged the architects of the amphitheater for choices that made it difficult to turn it into a town.

Codebases are like the amphitheater in Arles. Layers are written in one generation and modified later. Many people have touched the code. Tests are missing or enforce assumptions of a bygone era. Changing requirements have twisted the code's usage. Working with code is hard. It's also one of the first things you'll have to do.

This chapter will show you how to work with existing code. We'll introduce concepts that cause the mess—software entropy and technical debt—to give you some perspective. We'll then give practical guidance on how to safely change code, and we'll conclude with tips to avoid accidentally contributing to code clutter.

Software Entropy

As you explore code, you'll notice its shortcomings. Messy code is a natural side effect of change; don't blame developers for the untidiness. This drift toward disarray is known as *software entropy*.

Many things cause software entropy. Developers misunderstand each other's code or differ in style. Evolving technical stacks and product requirements cause chaos (see Chapter 11). Bug fixes and performance optimizations introduce complexity.

Luckily, software entropy can be managed. Code style and bug detection tools help keep code clean (Chapter 6). Code reviews help spread knowledge and reduce inconsistency (Chapter 7). Continuous refactoring reduces entropy (see "Changing Code" later in this chapter).

Technical Debt

Technical debt is a major cause of software entropy. Technical debt is future work that's owed to fix shortcomings in existing code. Like financial debt, technical debt has principal and interest. The principal is the original shortcoming that needs to be fixed. Interest is paid as code evolves without addressing the underlying shortcoming—increasingly complex workarounds are implemented. Interest compounds as the workarounds are replicated and entrenched. Complexity spreads, causing defects. Unpaid technical debt is common, and legacy code has a lot of it.

Technical decisions that you disagree with are not technical debt. Neither is code that you don't like. To be debt, the problem must require the team to "pay interest," or code must risk triggering a critical problem—one that requires urgent payment. Don't abuse the phrase. Saying "technical debt" too often will weaken the statement, making it harder to address important debt.

We know debt is frustrating, but it's not all bad. Martin Fowler divides technical debt into a two-by-two matrix (Table 3-1).

Table 3-1: Technical Debt Matrix

	RECKLESS	PRUDENT
DELIBERATE	"We don't have time for design."	"Let's ship now and deal with consequences."
INADVERTENT	"What's layering?"	"Now we know how we should've done it."

Source: *https://martinfowler.com/bliki/TechnicalDebtQuadrant.html*

Prudent, deliberate debt is the classic form of tech debt: a pragmatic trade-off between a known shortcoming in the code and speed of delivery. This is good debt as long as the team is disciplined about addressing it later.

Reckless, deliberate debt is created when teams are under pressure to deliver. "Just" is a hint that reckless debt is being discussed: "We can *just* add structured logging later," or, "*Just* increase the timeout."

Reckless, inadvertent debt comes from *unknown unknowns*. You can mitigate the danger of recklessly inadvertent debt by preemptively writing down and getting feedback on implementation plans and doing code reviews. Continuous learning also minimizes inadvertent recklessness.

Prudent, inadvertent debt is a natural outcome of growing experience. Some lessons are only learned in hindsight: "We should have created user accounts even for people who didn't complete the sign-up flow. Marketing needs to capture failed sign-ups, and now we have to add extra code that could've been avoided if it was part of the core data model." Unlike prudent and deliberate debt, the team will not know it's taking on debt. Unlike inadvertent, reckless debt, this type of debt is more of a natural outcome of learning about the problem domain or growing as a software architect—not the result of simply not doing one's homework. Healthy teams use practices such as project retrospectives to discover inadvertent debt and discuss when and whether to pay it down.

An important takeaway from this matrix is that some debt is unavoidable, as you can't prevent inadvertent mistakes. Debt might even be a mark of success: the project survived long enough to become messy.

Addressing Technical Debt

Don't wait until the world stops to fix problems for a month. Instead, clean things up and do minor refactoring as you go. Make changes in small, independent commits and pull requests.

You might find that incremental refactoring is insufficient—larger changes are needed. Large refactors are a serious commitment. In the short term, paying down debt slows feature delivery, while taking on more debt accelerates delivery. Long term, the opposite is true: paying down debt speeds up delivery, and taking on more slows delivery. Product managers are incentivized to push for more features (and thus, more debt). The right balance is highly context-dependent. If you have suggestions for large refactoring or rewriting, make the case to your team first. The following is a good framework for discussing technical debt:

1. State the situation factually.

2. Describe the risk and cost of the debt.

3. Propose a solution.

4. Discuss alternatives (including not taking action).

5. Weigh the trade-offs.

Make your proposal in writing. Do not base your appeal on a value judgment ("this code is old and ugly"). Focus on the cost of the debt and the benefit of fixing it. Be specific, and don't be surprised if you are asked to demonstrate the benefits after the work is done.

Hey all,

I think it's time we split the login service into two services: one for authentication and the other authorization.

Login service instability accounts for more than 30 percent of our on-call issues. The instability seems to come mostly from the intermingling of authentication and authorization logic. The current design makes it really difficult to test all of the security features we need to provide. We guarantee the safety of our customers' data, and the login service as is makes that an increasingly hard promise to keep. I haven't spoken with compliance, but I'm concerned that they'll raise an issue when we go through our next audit.

I think the access control logic was put in the service mostly out of expedience, given the various time and resource constraints at the time. There isn't an overarching architectural principle that led to this decision. Addressing it now, though, will mean refactoring the login service and moving the authorization code out—a big project. Still, I think it's worth it to fix the stability and correctness challenges.

One way to reduce the amount of work is to piggyback off of the backend team's authorization service instead of creating our own. I don't think this is the right approach because they're solving for a different set of use cases. We're dealing with user-facing authorization, while they're solving for system-to-system authorization. But maybe there's a nice way to handle both cleanly.

What do you think?

Thanks!
Johanna

Changing Code

Changing code is not like writing code in a fresh repository. You have to make changes without breaking existing behavior. You must understand what other developers were thinking and stick to existing styles and patterns. And you must gently improve the codebase as you go.

Code change techniques are largely the same, whether the change is adding new features, refactoring, deleting code, or fixing a bug. In fact, different types of changes are often combined. Refactoring—improving internal code structure without changing functionality—happens while adding a feature because it makes the feature easier to add. Code is deleted during a bug fix.

Changing large existing codebases is a skill refined over years—decades, even. The following tips will get you started.

Use the Legacy Code Change Algorithm

In his book *Working Effectively with Legacy Code* (Pearson, 2004), Michael C. Feathers proposes the following steps to safely modify existing codebases:

1. Identify change points.

2. Find test points.

3. Break dependencies.

4. Write tests.

5. Make changes and refactor.

Think of the first four steps as clearing space and building a fence around a field before planting seeds in step 5. Until the fence is up, wild animals can wander in and dig up your plants. Find the code you need to change and figure out how to test it. Refactor the code to make testing possible if needed. Add tests that validate existing behavior. Once the fence is up and the area around your change points is well protected, you can make changes on the inside.

First, locate the code that needs to be changed (the *change points*) using the strategies in Chapter 2: read the code, experiment, and ask questions. In our gardening metaphor, the change points are where you will plant your seeds.

Once you've located the code, find its test points. *Test points* are entry points into the code that you want to modify—the areas that tests invoke and inject into. Test points show code behavior before you change anything, and you'll need to use these points to test your own changes.

If you're lucky, the test points are easily accessible; if not, you'll need to break dependencies to get to them. In this context, dependencies aren't library or service dependencies; they are objects or methods that are required to test your code. *Breaking dependencies* means changing code structure so that it's easier to test. You will need to change the code to hook your tests up and supply synthetic inputs. These changes must *not* change behavior.

Refactoring to break dependences is the riskiest part of the work. It may even involve changing preexisting tests, which makes it harder to detect if behavior changed. Take small steps, and don't introduce any new functionality while in this phase. Make sure you can run tests quickly so you can run tests frequently.

A wide variety of techniques exist to break dependencies, including the following:

- Pulling apart a large, complex method into multiple smaller methods so separate pieces of functionality can be tested independently

- Introducing an interface (or other indirection) to give tests a way to supply a simple implementation of a complex object— incomplete, but sufficient for testing

- Injecting explicit control points that permit you to simulate aspects of execution that are hard to control, such as passage of time

Don't change access modifiers to make tests easier. Making private methods and variables public lets tests access code, but it also breaks encapsulation—a poor workaround. Breaking encapsulation increases the surface area of behavior you have to guarantee across the lifetime of the project. We discuss this more in Chapter 11.

As you refactor and break dependencies, add new tests to verify old behavior. Run the test suite frequently as you iterate, including both new and old tests. Consider using automated test tooling to generate tests that capture existing behaviors. See Chapter 6 for more on test writing.

Once dependencies are broken and good tests exist, it's time to make the "real" changes. Add tests that validate the changes, and then refactor code to further improve its design. You can make bold changes knowing you've secured the perimeter of the code.

Leave Code Cleaner Than You Found It

Coding lore on the internet often quotes the Boy Scout principle: "Always leave the campground cleaner than you found it." Like a campground, a codebase is shared, and it's nice to inherit a clean one. Applying the same philosophy to code—leave code cleaner than you found it—will help your code get better over time. No stop-the-world refactoring project is needed. The cost of refactoring will be amortized across many changes.

As you fix bugs or add features, clean adjacent code. Don't go out of your way to find dirty code. Be opportunistic. Try to keep the code-cleanup commits separate from your behavior-changing commits. Separating commits makes it easier to revert code changes without losing code-cleanup commits. Smaller commits also make changes easier to review.

Refactoring isn't the only way to clean code. Some code just stinks. Target smelly code as you go. *Code smell* is a term for code that isn't necessarily buggy but uses patterns known to cause problems; it "smells funny." Consider the following Java code snippet:

```
if (a < b)
    a += 1;
```

The snippet is perfectly correct. In Java, a single statement can follow a conditional without needing braces around it. However, the code is "smelly" because it makes it easy to make the following mistake down the line:

```
if (a < b)
    a += 1;
    a = a * 2;
```

Unlike Python, Java ignores indentation and relies on braces to group statements. So the a will be doubled regardless of the if condition. This mistake would be much harder to make if the optional braces surrounding a += 1; were used when the original code was written. The lack of braces is a code smell.

Many linters and code quality tools will detect this problem, as well as other code smells like really long methods or classes, duplicate code, excessive branching or looping, or having too many parameters. More subtle anti-patterns are harder to identify and correct without tooling and experience.

Make Incremental Changes

Refactoring often takes one of two forms. The first is a giant change-the-world code review that changes dozens of files at once. The second is a muddled pull request that has both refactoring and new features. Both types of changes are hard to review. Combined commits make it difficult to roll back functional changes without affecting refactoring you want to keep. Instead, keep your refactoring changes small. Make separate pull requests for each of the steps in the code change algorithm (see "Use the Legacy Code Change Algorithm" earlier). Use smaller commits if the changes are hard to follow. Finally, get buy-in from your team before you go on a refactoring spree. You're changing your team's code; they get to weigh in, too.

Be Pragmatic About Refactoring

It is not always wise to refactor. There are deadlines and competing priorities. Refactoring takes time. Your team might decide to ignore refactoring opportunities to ship new features. Such decisions add to the team's technical debt, which might be the right call. The cost of the refactor might also exceed its value. Old, deprecated code that's being replaced doesn't need to be refactored, nor does code that's low risk or rarely touched. Be pragmatic about when you refactor.

Use an IDE

Integrated development environments (IDEs) carry a stigma among 133t coders; they see getting "help" from an editor as a weakness and fetishize Vim or Emacs—"an elegant weapon for a more civilized age." This is nonsense. Take advantage of the tools that are available to you. If your language has a good IDE, use it.

IDEs are particularly helpful when refactoring. They have tools for renaming and moving code, extracting methods and fields, updating method signatures, and doing other common operations. In large codebases, simple code operations are both tedious and error prone. IDEs will automatically go through the code and update it to reflect the new changes. (To forestall the hate mail: we are aware of ways to get Vim and Emacs to do this, too.)

Just don't get carried away. IDEs make refactoring so easy that a few simple tweaks can create huge code reviews. A human still has to review your automated IDE changes. Automatic refactoring has its limits, too. A reference to a renamed method might not get adjusted if it is invoked through reflection or metaprogramming.

Use Version Control System Best Practices

Changes should be committed to a *version control system (VCS)*, such as Git. A VCS tracks the history of a codebase: who made each change (*commit*) and when it was made. A *commit message* is also attached to each commit.

Commit your changes early and often during development. Frequent commits show how code changes over time, let you undo changes, and act as a remote backup. However, frequently committing often leads to meaningless messages like "oops" or "fix broken test." There's nothing wrong with shorthand commit messages when you're cranking out code, but they're worthless to everyone else. Rebase your branch, squash your commits, and write a clear commit message before submitting a change for review.

Your squashed commit messages should follow your team's conventions. Prefixing commit messages with an issue ID is common: "[MYPROJ-123] Make the backend work with Postgres." Tying a commit to an issue lets developers find more context for the change and allows for scripting and tooling. Follow Chris Beams's advice (*https://chris.beams.io/posts/git-commit*) if there are no established rules:

- Separate subject from body with a blank line.
- Limit the subject line to 50 characters.
- Capitalize the subject line.
- Do not end the subject line with a period.
- Use the imperative mood in the subject line.
- Wrap the body at 72 characters.
- Use the body to explain what and why versus how.

Chris's post is worth a read; it describes good hygiene.

Avoiding Pitfalls

Existing code comes with baggage. Libraries, frameworks, and patterns are already in place. Some standards will bother you. It's natural to want to work with clean code and a modern tech stack, but the temptation to rewrite code or ignore standards is dangerous. Rewriting code can destabilize a codebase if not done properly, and rewrites come at the expense of new features. Coding standards keep code legible; diverging will make it hard on developers.

In his book *The Hard Thing About Hard Things* (Harper Business, 2014), Ben Horowitz says:

> *The primary thing that any technology startup must do is build a product that's at least ten times better at doing something than the current prevailing way of doing that thing. Two or three times better will not be good enough to get people to switch to the new thing fast enough or in large enough volume to matter.*

Ben is talking about startup products, but the same idea applies to existing code. If you want to rewrite code or diverge from standards, your improvement must be an order of magnitude better. Small gains aren't enough—the cost is too high. Most engineers underestimate the value of convention and overestimate the value of ignoring it.

Be careful about rewrites, breaking with convention, or adding new technology to the stack. Save rewrites for high-value situations. Use boring technology when possible. Don't ignore convention, even if you disagree with it, and avoid forking code.

Use Boring Technology

Software is a fast-moving field. New tools, languages, and frameworks come out constantly. Compared to what's online, existing code looks dated. However, successful companies have durable code with older libraries and older patterns for a reason: success takes time, and churning through technologies is a distraction.

The problem with new technology is that it's less mature. In his presentation "Choose Boring Technology," Dan McKinley points out, "Failure modes of boring technology are well understood" (*http://boringtechnology .club/*). All technology is going to break, but old stuff breaks in predictable ways. New things break in surprising ways. Lack of maturity means smaller communities, less stability, less documentation, and less compatibility. New technologies have fewer Stack Overflow answers.

Sometimes new technology will solve your company's problems, and sometimes it won't. It takes discipline and experience to discern when to use new technology. The benefit has to exceed the cost. Each decision to use new technology costs an "innovation token," a concept Dan uses to show that effort spent on new technologies could also be spent on innovative new features. Companies have a limited number of such tokens.

To balance the cost and benefit, spend your tokens on technologies that serve high-value areas (core competencies) of your company, solve a wide range of use cases, and can be adopted by multiple teams. If your company specializes in predictive analytics for mortgages and has a team of PhD data scientists, adopting bleeding-edge machine learning algorithms makes sense; if your company has 10 engineers and is building iOS games, use something off the shelf. New technology has a greater benefit if it makes your company more competitive. If it can be adopted widely, more teams will benefit, and your company will have less software to maintain overall.

Choosing a new programming language for a project has particularly far-reaching consequences. Using a new language pulls an entire technology stack into your company's ecosystem. New build systems, test frameworks, IDEs, and libraries must all be supported. A language might have major advantages: a particular programming paradigm, ease of experimentation, or eliminating some kinds of errors. A language's advantages have to be balanced against its trade-offs. If using a new framework or database costs one innovation token, a new language costs three.

The maturity of the ecosystem around a new language is particularly crucial. Is the build and packaging system well thought out? How is IDE support? Are important libraries maintained by experienced developers? Are test frameworks available? Can you pay for support if you need it? Can you hire engineers with relevant skills? How easy is the language to pick up? How does the language perform? Does the language ecosystem integrate with existing tools at the company? Answers to these questions are as important as the features of the language itself. Billion-dollar companies have been built on boring languages. Great software has been written in C, Java, PHP, Ruby, and .NET. Unless the language is dying, its age and lack of buzz are hardly arguments against it.

SBT AND SCALA

In 2009, LinkedIn developers discovered Scala. It was more pleasant to write code in Scala than Java, which LinkedIn used widely. It had a powerful, expressive type system. It was less verbose. It incorporated functional programming techniques. Moreover, Scala runs on the Java Virtual Machine (JVM), so the operations team could run Scala using the same JVM tools they were used to. It also meant that Scala code could interoperate with existing Java libraries. Several large projects adopted Scala, including LinkedIn's distributed graph and its new log system, Kafka.

Chris created a stream processing system for Kafka, called Samza. He quickly discovered that the theory of easy integration with the JVM didn't pan out in practice. Many Java libraries were clunky to use with Scala's collections libraries. On top of that, Scala's build environment was painful. LinkedIn was using Gradle as its build system—another nascent technology. Gradle didn't have any Scala support. The Scala community used the Scala Build Tool (SBT).

SBT is a build system built in Scala itself. It defined a domain-specific language (DSL) for creating build files. Chris learned that there were two entirely different DSLs for SBT, depending on which version you were running. Most of the examples on the internet used the older, abandoned syntax. The documentation for the new syntax was completely impenetrable to him.

Over the subsequent years, Scala continued to be a thorn in his side: binary incompatibility between versions, JVM segmentation faults, immature libraries, and lack of integration with LinkedIn internal tooling. The team began hiding Scala, stripping it out of client libraries. For someone like Chris, who was more focused on stream processing than language particulars, Scala circa 2011 turned out to have been a bad choice. It diverted a lot of his time to language and tooling problems. It just wasn't boring enough.

Don't Go Rogue

Don't ignore your company's (or industry's) standards because you don't like them. Writing nonstandard code means that it won't fit in with the company's environment. Continuous integration checks, IDE plugins, unit tests, code linting, log aggregation tools, metrics dashboards, and data pipelines are all integrated already. Your custom approach will be costly.

Your preferences might truly be better. Going rogue still isn't a good idea. In the short term, do what everyone else is doing. Try to understand the reasoning for the standard approach. It's possible that it is solving a nonobvious problem. If you can't figure out a good reason, ask around. If you still can't find an answer, start a conversation with your manager and the team that owns the technology.

There are many dimensions to consider when changing standards: priority, ownership, cost, and implementation details. Convincing a team to kill something that they own is not easy. There will be many opinions. You need to be pragmatic.

As with rewrites, changing something that's widely adopted is slow. This doesn't mean it's not worth doing. Good things will happen to you if you go through the proper channels. You'll be exposed to other parts of the organization, which is great for networking and promotions. You'll also get to be an early adopter on the new solution—you'll get to use the new thing first. By providing input, you'll get what you want. But don't get distracted from your daily work, and make sure your manager is aware you're spending time on these projects.

Don't Fork Without Committing Upstream

A *fork* is a complete, independent copy of another source code repository. It has its own trunk, branches, and tags. On a code-sharing platform like GitHub, forks are used before submitting a pull request to the upstream repository. Forking lets people who don't have write access to the main repository contribute to the project—a normal and healthy practice.

It is less healthy to fork with no intention of contributing changes back. This happens when there are disagreements about the direction of a project, the original project is abandoned, or it's hard to get changes merged into the main codebase.

Maintaining an internal company fork is particularly pernicious. Developers will tell each other that they'll contribute the changes back "later." This rarely happens. Minor tweaks that are not contributed upstream compound over time. Eventually, you're running an entirely different piece of software. Features and bug fixes become increasingly difficult to merge upstream. The team discovers that it has implicitly signed up to maintain an entire project. Some companies even fork their own open source projects because they don't contribute internal changes!

Resist the Temptation to Rewrite

Refactoring efforts often escalate into full-blown rewrites. Refactoring existing code is daunting; why not throw away the old system and rewrite everything from scratch? Consider rewrites a last resort. This is hard-won advice from years of experience.

Some rewrites are worth doing, but many are not. Be honest about your desire for a rewrite. Code written in a language or framework that you don't like is not a good reason. Rewrites should only be undertaken if the benefit exceeds the cost; they are risky, and their cost is high. Engineers always underestimate how long a rewrite will take. Migrations, in particular, are awful. Data needs to be moved. Upstream and downstream systems need to be updated. This can take years—or even decades.

Rewrites aren't always better, either. In his famous book *The Mythical Man-Month* (Addison-Wesley Professional, 1995), Fred Brooks coined the phrase "Second System Syndrome," which describes how simple systems get replaced by complex ones. The first system is limited in scope, since its creators don't understand the problem domain. The system does its job, but it is awkward and limited. The developers, who now have experience, see clearly where they went wrong. They set out to develop a second system with all the clever ideas they have. The new system is designed for flexibility—everything is configurable and injectable. Sadly, second systems are usually a bloated mess. If you set out to rewrite a system, be very cautious about overextending.

MIGRATING DUCK DUCK GOOSE

Twitter's internal A/B testing tool is called Duck Duck Goose, or DDG for short. The first version of DDG was created fairly early in the company's history. It began showing its age after a few years of skyrocketing company growth. Several of the most experienced engineers started toying with the idea of rebuilding it. They wanted to improve the system architecture, make it more reliable and maintainable, change languages from Apache Pig to Scala, and address other limitations (this was a few years after Chris's Samza story, and Twitter had devoted years of effort to make Scala stable at the company). Dmitriy got roped into managing a team formed around this effort. The team combined the old developers, the engineers with new ideas, and several others. They estimated one quarter to build and release the new system and a second quarter to retire the old.

In practice, it took a year to make DDGv2 stable enough to become the default, and another six months to retire the old DDG. The old codebase earned a lot of respect in the process. The layers of complexity in the code began to make sense. In the end, the new

(continued)

tool was superior to its predecessor in many ways. It stood its own test of time: it's now older than v1 was when it was replaced. But what was estimated by experienced engineers and managers to be a six-month project wound up taking 18—well over a million dollars in additional development costs. Difficult conversations with vice presidents had to be had: "No, really, Boss, it will be better. I just need another quarter, again." Of the original three developers who prototyped the rewrite, two left the company, and the third transferred teams by the time it was finished. Don't go into a rewrite thinking it'll be a breeze. It'll be a slog.

Do's and Don'ts

DO'S	DON'TS
DO refactor incrementally.	**DON'T** overuse the phrase "technical debt."
DO keep refactoring commits separately from feature commits.	**DON'T** make methods or variables public for testing purposes.
DO keep changes small.	**DON'T** be a language snob.
DO leave code cleaner than you found it.	**DON'T** ignore your company's standards and tools.
DO use boring technology.	**DON'T** fork codebases without committing upstream.

Level Up

We make extensive use of Michael C. Feathers's book *Working Effectively with Legacy Code* (Pearson, 2004). The book goes into far more detail than we can in a few pages. If you find yourself dealing with large and messy codebases, we recommend Michael's book. You might also find Jonathan Boccara's book helpful: *The Legacy Code Programmer's Toolbox* (LeanPub, 2019).

Martin Fowler has written a lot about refactoring. For shorter reads, his blog is a great place to find content. If you're interested in the canonical book on refactoring, he's written *Refactoring: Improving the Design of Existing Code* (Addison-Wesley Professional, 1999).

Finally, we must mention *The Mythical Man-Month* by Fred Brooks (Addison-Wesley Professional, 1995). This is a classic that every software engineer should read. It talks about how software projects run in practice. You'll be surprised at how much this book applies to your daily experiences on the job.

WRITING OPERABLE CODE

C ode does weird things when exposed to "the real world." Users are unpredictable. Networks are unreliable. Things go wrong. Production software has to keep working. Writing operable code helps you deal with the unforeseen. Operable code has built-in protection, diagnostics, and controls. Protect your system by programming defensively with safe and resilient coding practices. Safe code prevents many failures, and resilient code recovers when failures do occur. You also need to be able to see what's going on so you can diagnose failures. Expose logging, metrics, and call trace information for easy diagnostics. Finally, you need to control systems without rewriting code. An operable system has configuration parameters and system tools.

This chapter describes some best practices that will make your code easier to run in production. There's a lot of ground to cover, so we kept things dense. By the end, you'll be familiar with key concepts and tools you need to make your software operable. Moreover, operability comments are common in code reviews; this information will help you give and receive better feedback.

Defensive Programming

Well-defended code is an act of compassion for anyone who runs your code (including you!). Defensive code fails less often, and when it does, it is more likely to recover. Make your code safe and resilient. *Safe code* takes advantage of compile-time validation to avoid runtime failures. Use immutable variables, access modifiers to restrict scope, and static type-checkers to prevent bugs. At runtime, validate input to avoid surprises. *Resilient code* uses exception-handling best practices and handles failures gracefully.

Avoid Null Values

In many languages, variables without a value default to null (or nil, None, or some other variant thereof). Null pointer exceptions are a common occurrence. Stack traces prompt head-scratching and a "how could this variable not have been set?" investigation. Avoid null pointer exceptions by checking that variables aren't null, by using the null object pattern, and by using option types.

Perform null checks at the beginning of methods. Use NotNull annotations and similar language features when available. Validating up front that variables aren't null means that later code can safely assume that it's dealing with real values; this will keep your code cleaner and more legible.

The *null object pattern* uses objects in lieu of null values. An example of this pattern is a search method that returns an empty list instead of null when no objects are found. Returning an empty list allows callers to safely iterate over the results, without special code to handle empty result sets.

Some languages have built-in *option types*—Optional or Maybe—that force developers to think about how empty responses are handled. Take advantage of option types if they're available.

Make Variables Immutable

Immutable variables can't be changed once they're set. If your language has a way to explicitly declare variables as immutable (final in Java, val rather than var in Scala, let instead of let mut in Rust), do so whenever possible. Immutable variables prevent unexpected modifications. Many more variables can be made immutable than you might expect at first blush. As a bonus, using immutable variables makes parallel programming simpler, and a compiler or runtime that knows a variable is not going to change can be more efficient.

Use Type Hinting and Static Type Checking

Constrain the values that variables can take. For example, variables with only a few valid string values should be an Enum rather than a String. Constraining variables will ensure that unexpected values will immediately fail (or might not even compile) rather than cause bugs. Use the most specific type possible when defining variables.

Dynamic languages such as Python (starting with Python 3.5), Ruby via Sorbet (slated to be part of Ruby 3), and JavaScript (via TypeScript) all now have increasingly robust support for *type hinting* and *static type checkers*. Type hinting lets you specify a variable's type in a language that's normally dynamically typed. For example, the following Python 3.5 method uses type hinting to receive and return a string:

```
def say(something: str) -> str:
    return "You said: " + something
```

Best of all, type hinting can be added gradually to existing codebases. When combined with a static type checker, which uses type hints to find bugs before code is executed, you can prevent runtime failures.

Validate Inputs

Never trust the input your code receives. Developers, faulty hardware, and human error can mangle input data. Protect your code by validating that its input is well formed. Use preconditions, checksum and validate data, use security best practices, and use tools to find common errors. Reject bad input as early as possible.

Validate method input variables using preconditions and post-conditions. Use libraries and frameworks that validate preconditions when the type you use does not fully capture valid variable values. Most languages have libraries with methods like checkNotNull or annotations like @Size(min=0, max=100). Be as constrained as possible. Check that input strings match expected formats, and remember to deal with leading or trailing whitespace. Validate that all numbers are in appropriate ranges: if a parameter should be greater than zero, ensure that it is; if a parameter is an IP address, check that it's a valid IP.

NO WORD ALLOWED

Dmitriy worked part-time at a comparative genomics lab in college. His team built a web service for scientists to upload DNA sequences and run the lab's tools on them. One of the most common causes of errors they encountered was that biologists would put the text of the DNA sequence—a long string of As, Cs, Ts, and Gs—into a Word document rather than a simple text file. The parsers would of course break, and no results would be generated. The user was told that no matching sequence was found. This was a common occurrence. People filed bug reports suggesting that the DNA search was broken: it wasn't finding sequences that absolutely must be in the database.

This went on for quite some time. The team blamed the users because the directions clearly stated "plaintext file." Eventually, Dmitriy got tired of responding to the emails with instructions for saving a plaintext file, so he updated the site. Did he add a Word parser? Goodness no. Did he add file format checking and proper error instrumentation to alert the user that the site couldn't handle their submission? Of course not. He added a large Microsoft Word icon with a red line through it and a link to instructions. The support email volume went down drastically! Success!

The old website is still up, though it has been upgraded. The "No Word allowed!" icon is gone; just a warning remains: "Text files only. Word documents are not accepted." Fifteen years after leaving that job, Dmitriy tried uploading a Word document of a well-studied gene. No results were found; no errors returned. That's decades of misleading results because Dmitriy was too lazy to handle inputs properly. Don't be 20-year-old Dmitriy. He might have sabotaged a cure for cancer with this.

Computer hardware isn't always trustworthy. Networks and disks can corrupt data. If you need strong durability guarantees, use checksums to validate that data hasn't changed unexpectedly.

Don't overlook security, either. External inputs are dangerous. Malicious users might try to inject code or SQL into inputs, or overrun buffers to gain control of your application. Use mature libraries and frameworks to prevent cross-site scripting. Always escape inputs to prevent SQL injection attacks. Explicitly set size parameters when manipulating memory with commands like `strcpy` (specifically use `strncpy`) to prevent buffer overflows. Use widely adopted security and cryptography libraries or protocols instead of writing your own. Familiarize yourself with the Open Web Application Security Project (OWASP) Top 10 security report (*https://owasp.org/www-project-top-ten/*) to quickly bootstrap your security knowledge.

Use Exceptions

Don't use special return values (`null`, 0, –1, and so on) to signal an error. All modern languages support exceptions or have a standard exception-handling pattern (like Go's `error` type). Special values aren't obviously visible from a method signature. Developers won't know that error conditions are returned and need to be handled. It's also difficult to remember which return value corresponds to which failure state. Exceptions carry more information than a null or -1; they're named and have stack traces, line numbers, and messages.

For example, in Python a ZeroDivisionError returns a lot more information than a None return value:

```
Traceback (most recent call last):
  File "<stdin>", line 1, in <module>
ZeroDivisionError: integer division or modulo by zero
```

In many languages, checked exceptions are visible from method signatures:

```
// Go's Open method clearly has an error return
func Open(name string) (file *File, err error)

// Java's open() method clearly throws an IOException
public void open (File file) throws IOException
```

An error declaration in Go and an exception declaration in Java clearly signal that the open methods can raise errors that need to be handled.

Be Precise with Exceptions

Precise exceptions make code easier to use. Use built-in exceptions when possible and avoid creating generic exceptions. Use exceptions for failures, not to control application logic.

Most languages have built-in exception types (FileNotFoundException, AssertionError, NullPointerException, and so on). Don't create custom exceptions if a built-in type can describe the problem. Developers have experience with existing exception types and will know what they mean.

When creating your own exceptions, don't make them too generic. Generic exceptions are difficult to handle because developers don't know what kind of problem they're dealing with. If developers don't get a precise signal of the error that occurred, they'll be forced to fail the application—a significant action. Be as specific as possible about the exception types you raise so developers can react to failures appropriately.

Don't use exceptions for application logic, either. You want your code to be unsurprising, not clever. Using exceptions to break out of a method is confusing and makes code hard to debug.

This Python example uses `FoundNodeException` rather than directly returning the node that was found:

```python
def find_node(start_node, search_name):
    for node in start_node.neighbors:
        if search_name in node.name:
            raise FoundNodeException(node)
        find_node(node, search_name)
```

Don't do this. Just return the node.

Throw Exceptions Early, Catch Exceptions Late

Follow the "throw early, catch late" principle. *Throwing early* means raising exceptions as close to the error as possible so developers can quickly find the relevant code. Waiting to throw an exception makes it harder to find where the failure actually happened. When an error occurs but other code is executed before the exception is thrown, you risk the possibility of a second error being triggered. If an exception is thrown for the second error, you don't know that the first error happened. Tracking down this kind of bug is maddening. You fix a bug only to discover that the real problem was something upstream.

Catching exceptions late means propagating exceptions up the call stack until you reach the level of the program that is capable of handling the exception. Consider an application that tries to write to a full disk. There are many possible next steps: blocking and retrying, retrying asynchronously, writing to a different disk, alerting a human user, or even crashing. The appropriate reaction depends on application specifics. A database write-ahead log must be written, while a word processor's background save can be delayed. The piece of code that can make this decision is likely several layers removed from the low-level library that encounters a full disk. All the intermediate layers need to propagate the exception upward and not attempt premature remediation. The worst of premature remediation is "swallowing" an exception you can't address, usually by ignoring it in a catch block:

```
try {
  // ...
} catch (Exception e) {
  // ignoring since there's nothing I can do about it
}
```

This exception will not get logged or rethrown, nor will any other action be taken; it's completely ignored. The failure gets hidden, possibly to disastrous effect. When calling code that might throw exceptions, either handle them completely or propagate them up the stack.

Retry Intelligently

The appropriate reaction to an error is often to simply try again. Plan on occasionally having to try multiple times when calling remote systems. Retrying an operation sounds easy: catch the exception and retry the operation. In practice, when and how often to retry requires some know-how.

The most naïve retry approach is simply to catch an exception and retry the operation immediately. But what if the operation fails again? If a disk runs out of space, it's likely to be out of space 10 milliseconds later, and 10 milliseconds after that. Banging away over and over slows things down and makes it harder for the system to recover.

It's prudent to use a strategy called *backoff*. Backoff increases sleep time nonlinearly (usually using an exponential backoff, such as (retry number)^2). If you use this approach, make sure to cap the backoff at some maximum so it doesn't get too large. However, if a network server has a blip and all clients experience that blip simultaneously, then back off using the same algorithm; they will all reissue their requests at the same time. This is called a *thundering herd*; many clients issuing retry requests simultaneously can bring a recovering service back down. To handle this, add *jitter* to the backoff strategy. With jitter, clients add a random, bounded amount of time to the backoff. Introducing randomness spreads out the requests, reducing the likelihood of a stampede.

Don't blindly retry all failed calls, particularly ones that write data or cause some business process to execute. It is better to let the application crash when it encounters an error it was not designed to handle; this is called *failing fast*. If you fail fast, no further damage will be done, and a human can figure out the correct course of action. Make sure to fail not only fast but also loudly. Relevant information should be visible so that debugging is easy.

Write Idempotent Systems

It's not always obvious what state the system was left in after a failure. If the network fails during a remote write request, did the request succeed before the failure or not? This leaves you in a pickle: Do you retry and risk double-writing the request, or do you give up and risk losing the data? In a billing system, a retry might double-charge the customer, while not retrying might mean not charging them at all. Sometimes you can read the remote system to check, but not always. Local state mutations can suffer from similar problems. Nontransactional in-memory data structure mutations can leave your system in an inconsistent state.

The best way to deal with retries is to build idempotent systems. An *idempotent* operation is one that can be applied multiple times and still yield the same outcome. Adding a value to a set is idempotent. No matter how many times the value is added, it exists in the set once. Remote APIs can be made idempotent by allowing clients to supply a unique ID for each request. When a client retries, it supplies the same unique ID as its failed attempt; the server can then de-duplicate the request if it's already been processed. Making all your operations idempotent greatly simplifies system interactions and eliminates a large class of possible errors.

Clean Up Resources

Be sure to clean all resources when a failure occurs. Release memory, data structures, network sockets, and file handles that you no longer need. Operating systems have a fixed amount of space for file handles and network sockets; once exceeded, all new handles and sockets fail to open. Leaking network sockets—failing to close them after use—will keep useless connections alive, which will fill connection pools. The following code is dangerous:

```
f = open('foo.txt', 'w')
# ...
f.close()
```

Any failures that happen before f.close() will prevent the file pointer from being closed. If your language doesn't support auto-closing, wrap your code in a try/finally block to safely close file handles even if an exception occurs.

Many modern languages have features that automatically close resources. Rust will automatically close resources by invoking a destructor method when objects leave scope. Python's with statement automatically closes handles when the call path leaves the block:

```
with open('foo.txt') as f:
  # ...
```

Logging

The first time you wrote "Hello, world!" to a terminal, you were logging. Printing log messages is simple and convenient for understanding code or debugging a small program. For complex applications, languages have sophisticated logging libraries to give operators more control over what's logged and when. Operators can modulate log volume through logging levels and control log formats. Frameworks also inject contextual information—thread names, hostnames, IDs—that you can use when debugging. Logging frameworks work well with log management systems, which aggregate log messages so operators can filter and search them.

Use a logging framework to make your code easier to operate and debug. Set log levels so your operators can control your application's log volume. Keep logs atomic, fast, and secure.

Use Log Levels

Logging frameworks have *log levels*, which let operators filter messages based on importance. When an operator sets a log level, all logs at or above the level will be emitted, while messages from lower levels will be silenced. Levels are usually controlled through both a global setting and package or class-level overrides. Log levels let operators adjust log volume as befits a given situation, from extremely detailed debugging logs to a steady background hum of normal operations.

For example, here's a Java `log4j.properties` snippet that defines an ERROR-level root verbosity and a package-specific INFO-level verbosity for logs coming from the `com.foo.bar` package space:

```
# set root logger to ERROR level for fout FileAppender
log4j.rootLogger=ERROR,fout

# set com.foo.bar to INFO level
log4j.logger.com.foo.bar=INFO
```

You must use the appropriate criticality for each log message for log levels to be useful. While log levels are not completely standard, the following levels are common:

TRACE   This is an extremely fine level of detail that only gets turned on for specific packages or classes. This is rarely used outside of development. If you need line-by-line logs or data structure dumps, this level is for you. If you find yourself using TRACE frequently, you should consider using a debugger to step through code instead.

DEBUG This is used when the message will be useful during a production issue but not during normal operations. Don't use debug-level logging so much that the output is unusable when debugging; save that for TRACE.

INFO This is nice-to-have information about the state of the application but not indicative of any problems. Application state messages like "Service started" and "Listening on port 5050" go here. INFO is the default log level. Don't emit frivolous logs with INFO— "just in case" logging goes into TRACE or DEBUG. INFO logging should tell us something useful during normal operations.

WARN These are messages about potentially problematic situations. A resource nearing its capacity merits a warning. Whenever you log a warning, there should be a concrete action you want the person seeing the message to take. If the warning is not actionable, log it to INFO.

ERROR These messages indicate that an error that needs attention is occurring. An unwritable database usually merits an ERROR log. ERROR logs should be detailed enough to diagnose problems. Log explicit details, including relevant stack traces and the resulting actions the software is performing.

FATAL These are the "last gasp" log messages. If the program encounters a condition so severe that it must exit immediately, a message about the cause of the problem can be logged at the FATAL level. Include relevant context about the program's state; locations of recovery or diagnostic-related data should be logged.

Here's an INFO-level log emitted in Rust:

```
info!("Failed request: {}, retrying", e);
```

The log line includes the error that causes the request to fail. The INFO level is used because the application is automatically retrying; no operator action is needed.

Keep Logs Atomic

If information is useful only when coupled with other data, log it all *atomically* in one message. Atomic logs, which have all relevant information in one line, work better with log aggregators. Don't assume that logs will be seen in a specific order; many operational tools reorder or even drop messages. Don't rely on system clock timestamps for ordering: system clocks can get reset or drift between hosts. Avoid newlines in log messages; many log aggregators treat each new line as a separate message. Make extra sure that stack traces are logged in a single message, as they often include newlines when printed.

Here's an example of nonatomic log messages:

```
2022-03-19 12:18:32,320 – appLog – WARNING – Request failed with:
2022-03-19 12:18:32,348 – appLog – INFO – User login: 986
Unable to read from pipe.
2022-03-19 12:18:32,485 – appLog – INFO – User logout: 986
```

The WARNING log message has a newline in it, which makes it hard to read. Subsequent lines from the WARNING have no timestamp and are intermingled with other INFO messages coming from another thread. The WARNING should have been written atomically as one line.

If log messages can't be output atomically, include a unique ID in the messages so they can be stitched together later.

Keep Logs Fast

Excessive logging will hurt performance. Logs must be written somewhere—to disk, to a console, or to a remote system. Strings must be concatenated and formatted before they're written. Use parameterized logging and asynchronous appenders to keep logging fast.

You'll find string concatenation is very slow and can be devastating in performance-sensitive loops. When a concatenated string is passed into a log method, the concatenation happens regardless of the verbosity level because arguments are evaluated before they're passed into a method. Log frameworks provide mechanisms to delay string concatenation until it's actually needed. Some frameworks force log messages into closures that aren't evaluated unless a log line is invoked, while others provide support parameterized messages.

For example, Java has three ways to concatenate strings in log calls, two of which concatenate the string parameter before calling the `trace` method:

```
while(messages.size() > 0) {
  Message m = message.poll();

  // This string is concatenated even when trace is disabled!
  log.trace("got message: " + m);

  // This string is also concatenated when trace is disabled.
  log.trace("got message: {}".format(m));

  // This string is only concatenated when trace is enabled. It's faster.
  log.trace("got message: {}", m);
}
```

The final call uses a parameterized string that will be evaluated only if the log line is actually written.

You can also manage performance impact using *appenders*. Appenders route logs to different locations: the console, a file, or a remote log aggregator. Default log appenders usually operate in the caller's thread, the same way a call to `print` would. *Asynchronous* appenders write log messages without blocking execution threads. This improves performance since application code doesn't need to wait for logs to be written. *Batching* appenders buffer log messages in-memory before writing to disk, thus improving write throughput. The operating system's page cache helps log throughput by acting as a buffer as well. While asynchronous and batching writes improve performance, they can result in lost log messages if an application crashes, since not all logs are guaranteed to be flushed to disk.

Beware that changing log verbosity and configuration can eliminate race conditions and bugs because it slows down the application. If you enable verbose logging to debug an issue and discover a bug disappears, the logging change itself might be the reason.

Don't Log Sensitive Data

Be careful when dealing with sensitive data. Log messages shouldn't include private data like passwords, security tokens, credit card numbers, or emails. This might seem obvious, but it's easy to get wrong—simply logging a URL or HTTP response can expose information that log aggregators are not set up to safeguard. Most frameworks support rule-based string replacement and redaction; configure them, but do not rely on them as your only defense. Be paranoid; logging sensitive data can create security risks and violate privacy regulations.

Metrics

Instrument your application with metrics to see what it is doing. Metrics are the numerical equivalent of logs; they measure application behavior. How long did a query take? How many elements are in a queue? How much data was written to disk? Measuring application behavior helps detect problems and is useful for debugging.

There are three common metric types: counters, gauges, and histograms. These names are similar, but not consistent, across different monitoring systems. *Counters* measure the number of times an event happens. Using a cache hit counter and a request counter, you can calculate cache hit rates. Counters only increase in value or reset to 0 when a process restarts (they are *monotonically increasing*). *Gauges* are point-in-time measurements that can go up or down; think of a speedometer or a gas volume indicator in a car. Gauges expose statistics such as the size of a queue, stack, or map. *Histograms* break events into ranges based on their magnitude. Each range has a counter that is incremented whenever an event value falls into its range. Histograms commonly measure the amount of time requests take, or data payload sizes.

System performance is often measured in terms of metric values at threshold percentiles—for example, the 99th percentile, referred to as *P99*. A system with a 2-millisecond P99 latency takes 2 milliseconds or less to respond to 99 percent of the requests it receives. Percentiles are derived from histograms. To cut down on the data that needs to be tracked, some systems require you to configure which percentiles you care about; if a system tracks P95 by default but you have a P99 service level objective (SLO), make sure to change settings accordingly.

Application metrics are aggregated into centralized *observability systems* like Datadog, LogicMonitor, or Prometheus. Observability is a concept from control theory that defines how easy it is to determine the state of a system by looking at its outputs. Observability systems try to make it easier to determine a running application's state by providing dashboards and monitoring tools on top of aggregated metrics. Dashboards show operators what's going on in the system, and monitoring tools trigger alerts based on metric values.

Metrics are also used to automatically scale a system up or down. *Autoscaling* is common in environments that provide dynamic resource allocation. For example, cloud hosts may automatically adjust the number of running instances by monitoring load metrics. Autoscaling increases server capacity when it is needed and reduces server capacity to save money later.

To track SLOs, use observability systems, and take advantage of autoscaling features, you must measure everything. Metrics are tracked using a standard metrics library; most application frameworks provide these. As a developer, it is your job to ensure that important metrics are exposed to observability systems.

Use Standard Metrics Libraries

While counters, gauges, and histograms are pretty easy to calculate, don't roll your own metrics library. Nonstandard libraries are a maintenance nightmare. Standard libraries will integrate with everything out of the box. Your company probably has a metrics library that they prefer. If they do, use it. If they don't, start a discussion to adopt one.

Most observability systems offer metric client libraries in a range of languages. We'll use a StatsD client in a simple Python web application to show what metrics look like. Metrics libraries all look pretty similar, so our example should translate nearly verbatim to whichever library you use.

The Python web application in Listing 4-1 has four methods: set, get, unset, and dump. The methods set and get simply set and retrieve values in a map stored in the service. The unset method deletes key-value pairs from the map and dump JSON-encodes the map and returns it.

```python
import json
from flask import Flask, jsonify
from statsd import StatsClient

app = Flask(__name__)
statsd = StatsClient()
map = {}

@app.route('/set/<k>/<v>')
def set(k, v):
    """ Sets a key's value. Overwrites if key already exists. """
    map[k] = v
    statsd.gauge('map_size', len(map))

@app.route('/get/<k>')
def get(k):
    """ Returns key's value if it exists. Else, None is returned. """
    try:
        v = map[k]
        statsd.incr('key_hit')

        return v
    except KeyError as e:
        statsd.incr('key_miss')
```

```
    return None

@app.route('/unset/<k>')
def unset(k):
    """ Deletes key from map if it exists. Else, no-op. """
    map.pop(k, None)
    statsd.gauge('map_size', len(map))

@app.route('/dump')
def dump():
    """ Encodes map as a JSON string and returns it. """
    with statsd.timer('map_json_encode_time'):
        return jsonify(map)
```

Listing 4-1: *An example Python Flask application using the StatsD client metrics library*

This example uses counters key_hit and key_miss to track hits and misses in get with statsd.incr. A timer (statsd.timer) measures how long it takes to encode the map into JSON, which will be added to a timing histogram. Serialization is a costly, CPU-intensive operation, so it should be measured. A gauge (statsd.gauge) measures the current size of the map. We could have used increment and decrement methods on a counter to track the map size, but using a gauge is less error prone.

Web application frameworks like Flask usually do a lot of metric calculations for you. Most will count all HTTP status codes for every method invocation in the web service and time all HTTP requests. Framework metrics are a great way to get a ton of metrics for free; just configure the framework to output to your observability system. Plus, your code will be cleaner since measurement happens underneath.

Measure Everything

Measurements are cheap; you should use them extensively. Measure all of the following data structures, operations, and behaviors:

- Resource pools
- Caches
- Data structures

- CPU-intensive operations

- I/O-intensive operations

- Data size

- Exceptions and errors

- Remote requests and responses

Use gauges to measure the size of resource pools. Pay special attention to thread pools and connection pools. Large pools are an indication that the system is stuck or unable to keep up.

Count cache hits and misses. Shifts in the hit-to-miss ratio impact application performance.

Measure the size of key data structures with gauges. Abnormal data structure size is an indication that something strange is going on.

Time CPU-intensive operations. Pay special attention to data serialization operations, which are surprisingly expensive. A simple JSON-encode of a data structure is often the costliest operation in code.

Disk and network I/O operations are slow and unpredictable. Use timers to measure how long they take. Measure the size of the data that your code deals with. Track the size of *remote procedure call (RPC)* payloads. Track the size of data generated for I/O using histograms (similar to timers) so you can see 99th percentile data sizes. Large data has an impact on memory footprint, I/O speed, and disk usage.

Count every exception, error response code, and bad input. Measuring errors makes it easy to trigger an alert when things go wrong.

Measure any requests to your application. An abnormally high or low request count is a sign that something is amiss. Users want your systems to respond quickly, so you need to measure latency. Time all responses so you know when your system is slow.

Take time to understand how your metrics library works. It's not always obvious how a library calculates a metric; many libraries will sample measurements. Sampling keeps performance fast and reduces disk and memory usage, but it also makes measurements less accurate.

Traces

Developers all know about stack traces, but there's a less familiar kind of trace: a *distributed call trace*. A single call to a frontend API might result in hundreds of downstream RPC calls to different services. Distributed call traces stitch all of these downstream calls together into one graph. Distributed traces are useful for debugging errors, measuring performance, understanding dependencies, and analyzing system cost (which APIs are the most expensive to serve, which customers cost the most, and so on).

RPC clients use a tracing library to attach a call-trace ID to their request. Subsequent RPC calls by downstream services attach the same call-trace ID. Services then report the invocations that they receive along with the call-trace ID and other data, such as metadata tags and processing time. A dedicated system records all these reports and stitches call traces back together by call-trace ID. With this knowledge, the tracing system can present full distributed call graphs.

Call-trace IDs are usually propagated for you automatically through RPC client wrappers and service meshes. Verify that you're propagating any required state as you make calls to other services.

Configuration

Applications and services should expose settings that allow developers or site reliability engineers (SREs) to configure runtime behavior. Applying configuration best practices will make your code easier to run. Don't get too creative; use a standard configuration format, provide sensible defaults, validate configuration inputs, and avoid dynamic configuration when possible.

Configuration can be expressed in many ways:

- Files in plain, human-readable formats such as INI, JSON, or YAML
- Environment variables
- Command line flags

- A custom *domain-specific language (DSL)*

- The language the application is written in

Human-readable config files, environment variables, and command line flags are the most common approaches. Files are used when there are many values to set or there's a desire to version control the configurations. Environment variables are easy to set in scripts, and environments can be easily examined and logged. Command line flags are easy to set and are visible in process lists like ps.

DSLs are helpful when configuration needs programmable logic, like for loops or if statements. DSL-based configuration is commonly used when an application is written in a DSL-friendly language (like Scala). Using a DSL rather than a full-blown programming language, authors can provide shortcuts for complex operations and limit configurations to safe values and types—an important consideration for security and startup performance. But DSLs are hard to parse using standard tools, which makes interoperability with other tools difficult.

Expressing configuration in the application's language usually happens when the application is written in a scripting language like Python. Using code to generate configuration is powerful but also dangerous. Customizable logic obscures the configuration the application is seeing.

Don't Get Creative with Configuration

Configuration systems should be boring. An operator paged at 3 AM shouldn't need to remember Tcl syntax to change a timeout value.

Innovating on a configuration system is tempting. Configuration is familiar to everyone, and simple configuration systems seem to miss useful features—variable substitution, if statements, and so on. Many creative and well-meaning people have spent incredible amounts of time making fancy configuration systems. Sadly, the cleverer your configuration scheme is, the more bizarre your bugs will be. Do not get creative with configuration—use the simplest possible approach that will work. A static configuration file in a single standard format is ideal.

Most applications are configured through a static configuration file. Changing the file while the application is running won't affect the application; to pick up changes, the application needs to be restarted. Dynamic configuration systems are used when an application needs to be reconfigured without restarting. Dynamic configuration is typically stored in a dedicated configuration service, which gets polled or pushed by the application when values change. Alternatively, dynamic configuration is refreshed by periodically checking a local config file for updates.

Dynamic configuration is usually not worth the complexity it introduces. You need to think through all the implications of various configurations changing midflight. It also makes it harder to track when configuration was changed, who changed it, and what the value used to be—information that can be critical when debugging operational issues. It can also add external dependencies on other distributed systems. It sounds rudimentary, but restarting a process to pick up a new configuration is usually operationally and architecturally superior.

There are some common use cases that do warrant dynamic configuration, though. Log verbosity is frequently a dynamic setting. Operators can change the log level to a higher verbosity like DEBUG when something strange is going on. Restarting a process when odd behavior surfaces might change the behavior that you're trying to observe. Flipping a running process's log level lets you peek into its behavior without restarting.

Log and Validate All Configuration

Log all (nonsecret) configuration immediately upon startup to show what the application is seeing. Developers and operators occasionally misunderstand where a configuration file is supposed to be placed or how multiple configuration files get merged. Logging config values shows users whether the application is seeing the expected configuration.

Always validate configuration values when they're loaded. Do the validation only once, as early as possible (right after the configuration is loaded). Make sure that the values are set to the proper types, such as an integer for a port, and check that values make logical sense: check boundaries, string length, valid enum values, and so on. -200 is an integer but not a valid port. Take advantage of configuration systems that have robust type systems to express acceptable configuration values.

Provide Defaults

If a user has to set a large number of configuration parameters, your system will be hard to run. Set good defaults so your application will work well for most users out of the box. Default to network ports greater than 1024 (lower ports are restricted) if no port is configured. Use the system's temporary directory or the user's home directory if directory paths are unspecified.

Group Related Configuration

It's easy for application configuration to grow unmanageable, especially key-value formats that don't support nested configuration. Use a standard format like YAML that allows for nesting. Grouping related properties makes configuration easier to organize and maintain.

Combine tightly coupled parameters (like timeout duration and unit) in a single structure so the relationship is clear, and force the operator to declare the values atomically. Rather than defining `timeout _duration=10` and `timeout_units=second`, use `timeout=10s` or `""timeout""`: `{ ""duration"": 10, ""units"": ""second"" }`.

Treat Configuration as Code

The *configuration as code (CAC)* philosophy says that configuration should be subjected to the same rigor as code. Configuration mistakes can be disastrous. A single incorrect integer or missing parameter can break an application.

To keep configuration changes safe, configuration should be version controlled, reviewed, tested, built, and published. Keep configuration in a VCS like Git so you have a history of changes. Review configuration changes just like code reviews. Validate that configuration is properly formatted and conforms to expected types and value bounds. Build and publish configuration packages. We cover more on config delivery in Chapter 8.

Keep Configuration Files Clean

Clean configuration is easier for others to understand and change. Delete unused configuration, use standard formatting and spacing, and don't blindly copy configuration from other files (an example of *cargo culting*: copying things without actually understanding what they do or how they work). Tidy configuration is hard to maintain when you're iterating quickly, but misconfiguration causes production outages.

Don't Edit Deployed Configuration

Avoid hand-editing configuration on a specific machine. One-off config changes are overwritten on subsequent deployments, it's unclear who made the changes, and machines with similar configuration end up diverging.

As with keeping configuration files clean, resisting the temptation to hand-edit a config file in production is difficult, and in some cases unavoidable. If you edit configuration manually during a production incident, make sure changes get committed to the source of truth (the VCS) later.

Tools

Operable systems come with tools that help operators run the application. Operators might need to bulk-load data, run a recovery, reset database state, trigger a leadership election, or shift a partition assignment from one machine to another. Systems should come with tools to help operators deal with common operations.

Tool writing is collaborative. In some cases, you will be expected to write and supply operations tools. Organizations with strong SRE teams might also write tools for your systems. Regardless, work with your operations team to understand what they need.

SREs will usually prefer CLI-based tools and self-describing APIs since they are easily scriptable. Scriptable tools are easy to automate. If you plan on building UI-based tools, abstract the logic into a shared library or service that CLI-based tools can use as well. And treat your system's tools as code like any other: follow clean coding standards and test rigorously.

Your company might already have an existing toolset; it's common to have a standard internal web tools framework, for example. Integrate your tools with the standard frameworks available to you. Look for *single panes of glass* (unified management consoles). Companies with unified management consoles will expect all tools to be integrated with it. If your company has existing CLI-based tools, ask if it makes sense to integrate your tools with them. Everyone is used to the existing tool interfaces; integrating with them will make your tools easier to work with.

AMAZON BRINGS DOWN THE INTERNET

On February 28, 2017, Chris was in a meeting room in the office when he noticed that the meeting scheduling software, Zoom, stopped working. Not thinking much of it, he found himself back at his desk a few minutes later. He noticed that several major websites were acting funny. At this point, he heard from the operations team that Amazon Web Services (AWS) was having issues with its S3 storage system. Many large websites depend on Amazon, and Amazon depends heavily on S3. This was impacting basically the entire internet. Twitter began to fill with "Guess it's a snow day" and "Time to go home."

Amazon eventually posted a note describing what happened. An operations team was investigating a billing subsystem. An engineer executed a command to remove a small number of

(continued)

machines from the S3 billing pool. The engineer "fat fingered" (made a typo in) the node-count parameter. A lot more machines than intended were removed from the node pool, which triggered a full restart in several other critical subsystems. Eventually, this cascaded to a multihour outage that impacted many other top-tier companies.

Amazon's note has this brief, but telling, comment: "We are making several changes as a result of this operational event. While removal of capacity is a key operational practice, in this instance, the tool used allowed too much capacity to be removed too quickly. We have modified this tool to remove capacity more slowly and added safeguards to prevent capacity from being removed when it will take any subsystem below its minimum required capacity level. This will prevent an incorrect input from triggering a similar event in the future. We are also auditing our other operational tools to ensure we have similar safety checks."

Do's and Don'ts

DO'S	DON'TS
DO prefer compilation errors to run-time errors.	**DON'T** use exceptions for application logic.
DO make things immutable whenever possible.	**DON'T** use return codes for exception handling.
DO validate inputs and outputs.	**DON'T** catch exceptions that you can't handle.
DO study the OWASP Top 10.	**DON'T** write multiline logs.
DO use bug-checking tools and types or type hinting.	**DON'T** write secrets or sensitive data to logs.
DO clean up resources after exceptions (especially sockets, file pointers, and memory).	**DON'T** manually edit configuration on a machine.

DO'S	DON'TS
DO instrument your code with metrics.	**DON'T** store passwords or secrets in configuration files.
DO make your application configurable.	**DON'T** write custom configuration formats.
DO validate and log all configuration.	**DON'T** use dynamic configuration if you can avoid it.

Level Up

There aren't many books dedicated to writing operable code. Instead, these subjects appear in chapters throughout many software engineering books. Chapter 8 of Steve McConnell's *Code Complete* (Microsoft Press, 2004) covers defensive programming. Chapters 7 and 8 of *Clean Code* by Robert C. Martin (Pearson, 2008) cover error handling and boundaries. These are good places to start.

The web also has a lot of writing on defensive programming, exceptions, logging, configuration, and tooling. The *Amazon Builders' Library* (*https://aws.amazon.com/builders-library/*) from Amazon is a particularly useful resource.

Google SRE group's *Building Secure & Reliable Systems* (O'Reilly Media, 2020) is a treasure trove of sound advice, particularly from a security point of view. Google's *Site Reliability Engineering* (O'Reilly Media, 2016) is the canonical book on all things site reliability related. It's less focused on *writing* operable code, but it's still a must-read. It will give you a glimpse into the complex world of running production software. Both are available for free online, as well as in print.

MANAGING DEPENDENCIES

I n March 2016, thousands of JavaScript projects began failing to compile when a single package, left-pad, disappeared. The left-pad was a library with a single method that simply left-padded a string to a specific character width. Several foundational JavaScript libraries depended on left-pad. In turn, many projects depended on these libraries. Thanks to the viral nature of transitive dependencies, thousands and thousands of open source and commercial codebases had a critical dependency on this fairly trivial library. When the package was removed from NPM (JavaScript's Node Package Manager), a lot of programmers had a rough day.

Adding a dependency on existing code seems like a simple decision. Don't repeat yourself (DRY) is a commonly taught principle. Why should we all write our own left-pad? Database drivers, application frameworks, machine learning packages—there are many examples of libraries you should not write from scratch. But dependencies bring risk: incompatible changes, circular dependencies, version conflicts, and lack of control. You must consider these risks and how to mitigate them.

In this chapter, we cover the basics of dependency management and talk about every engineer's nightmare: dependency hell.

Dependency Management Basics

Before we can talk about problems and best practices, we must introduce you to common dependency and versioning concepts.

A *dependency* is code that your code relies on. The time at which a dependency is needed—during compilation, testing, or runtime—is called its *scope*.

Dependencies are declared in package management or build files: Java's Gradle or Maven configs, Python's *setup.py* or *requirements.txt*, and JavaScript's NPM *package.json*. Here is a snippet of a Java project's *build.gradle* file:

```
dependencies {
    compile 'org.apache.httpcomponents:httpclient:4.3.6'
    compile 'org.slf4j:slf4j-api:1.7.2'
}
```

The project depends on version 4.3.6 of an HTTP client library and version 1.7.2 of an SLF4J application programming interface (API) library. Each dependency is declared with a `compile` scope, meaning the dependencies are needed to compile the code. Each package has a version defined: 4.3.6 for `httpclient` and 1.7.2 for `slf4j`. Versioned packages are used to control when dependencies change and to resolve conflicts when different versions of the same package appear (more on this later).

A good versioning scheme has versions that are

UNIQUE   Versions should never be reused. Artifacts get distributed, cached, and pulled by automated workflows. Never republish changed code under an existing version.

COMPARABLE   Versions should help humans and tools reason about version precedence. *Precedence* is used to resolve conflicts when a build depends on multiple versions of the same artifact.

INFORMATIVE Versions differentiate between prereleased and released code, associate build numbers to artifacts, and set stability and compatibility expectations.

Git hashes or "marketing-related" versions like Android OS's dessert series (Android Cupcake, Android Froyo) or Ubuntu's alliterative animals (Trusty Tahr, Disco Dingo) satisfy the uniqueness property, but they are not comparable or informative. Similarly, a monotonically increasing version number (1, 2, 3) is both unique and comparable, but not terribly informative.

Semantic Versioning

The packages in the previous example use a versioning scheme called *semantic versioning (SemVer)*, one of the most commonly used versioning schemes. The official SemVer specification is available at *https://semver .org/*. The spec defines three numbers: the major, minor, and patch version (sometimes called the *micro version*). Version numbers are combined into a single MAJOR.MINOR.PATCH version number. The httpclient version 4.3.6 has a major, minor, and patch of 4, 3, and 6, respectively.

Semantic versions are unique, comparable, and informative. Each version number is used once and can be compared by going left to right (2.13.7 is before 2.14.1). They provide information about compatibility between different versions and can optionally encode release candidate or build number information.

Major version 0, considered "prerelease," is intended for fast iteration; no compatibility guarantees are made. Developers can change APIs in ways that break older code, like adding a new required parameter or deleting a public method. Starting with major version 1, a project is expected to guarantee the following:

- Patch versions are incremented for backward-compatible bug fixes.

- Minor versions are incremented for backward-compatible features.

- Major versions are incremented for backward-incompatible changes.

SemVer also defines prerelease versions by appending a - character after the patch version. Dot-separated alphanumeric sequences are used for prerelease identifiers (2.13.7-alpha.2). Prereleases can make breaking changes without bumping the major version. Many projects use *release candidate (RC)* builds. Early adopters can find bugs in RCs before the official release. RC prerelease versions have incremental identifiers, such as 3.0.0-rc.1. The final RC is then promoted to the release version by re-releasing it without an RC suffix. All prereleased versions are superseded by the final release (3.0.0 in our example). See Chapter 8 for more on release management mechanics.

Build numbers are appended after both the version and prerelease metadata: 2.13.7-alpha.2+1942. Including a build number helps developers and tools find the build logs for any version that was compiled.

SemVer's scheme also allows for *wildcard* version ranges (2.13.*). Since SemVer promises compatibility across minor and patch versions, builds should continue to work even as updated versions with bug fixes and new features are automatically pulled in.

Transitive Dependencies

Package management or build files show a project's direct dependencies, but direct dependencies are only a subset of what build or packaging systems actually use. Dependencies usually depend on other libraries, which become *transitive dependencies*. A dependency report shows the fully resolved *dependency tree* (or *dependency graph*). Most build and packaging systems can produce dependency reports. Continuing the previous example, here's the gradle dependencies output:

```
compile - Compile classpath for source set 'main'.
+--- org.apache.httpcomponents:httpclient:4.3.6
|    +--- org.apache.httpcomponents:httpcore:4.3.3
|    +--- commons-logging:commons-logging:1.1.3
|    \--- commons-codec:commons-codec:1.6
\--- org.slf4j:slf4j-api:1.7.2
```

The dependency tree shows the dependencies that the build system is actually using when it compiles the project. The report is several layers deep. Dependencies of dependencies of dependencies get pulled in, and so on. The httpclient library pulls in three transitive dependencies: httpcore, commons-logging, and commons-codec. The project does not depend directly on these libraries, but through httpclient, it does.

Understanding transitive dependencies is a critical part of dependency management. Adding a single dependency seems like a small change, but if that library depends on 100 others, your code now depends on 101 libraries. Any change in any dependency can affect your program. Make sure you know how to get information like the dependency tree in our examples so you can debug dependency conflicts.

Dependency Hell

Ask any software engineer about dependency hell, and you'll get a tale of woe. Conflicting versions of the same library, or an incompatible library upgrade, can break builds and cause runtime failures. The most common dependency hell culprits are circular dependencies, diamond dependencies, and version conflicts.

The previous dependency report was simple. A more realistic report will show version conflicts, and give you a glimpse of dependency hell:

```
compile - Compile classpath for source set 'main'.
+--- com.google.code.findbugs:annotations:3.0.1
|    +--- net.jcip:jcip-annotations:1.0
|    \--- com.google.code.findbugs:jsr305:3.0.1
+--- org.apache.zookeeper:zookeeper:3.4.10
|    +--- org.slf4j:slf4j-api:1.6.1 -> 1.7.21
|    +--- org.slf4j:slf4j-log4j12:1.6.1
|    +--- log4j:log4j:1.2.16
|    +--- jline:jline:0.9.94
|    \--- io.netty:netty:3.10.5.Final
\--- com.mycompany.util:util:1.4.2
     \--- org.slf4j:slf4j-api:1.7.21
```

This tree shows three direct dependencies: annotations, zookeeper, and util. The libraries all depend on other libraries; these are their transitive dependencies. Two versions of slf4j-api appear in the report. The util depends on slf4j-api version 1.7.21, but zookeeper depends on slf4j-api version 1.6.1.

The dependencies form a *diamond dependency*, illustrated in Figure 5-1.

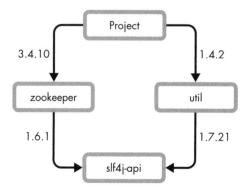

Figure 5-1: *A diamond dependency*

A project can't use two library versions simultaneously, so the build system must pick one. In a Gradle dependency report, version choices are shown with annotations like so:

```
|    +--- org.slf4j:slf4j-api:1.6.1 -> 1.7.21
```

The 1.6.1 -> 1.7.21 means that slf4j-api was upgraded to 1.7.21 across the whole project to resolve the version conflict. Zookeeper might not work correctly with a different version of slf4j-api, especially since a related dependency, slf4j-log4j12, did not get upgraded. The upgrade *should* work, since Zookeeper dependency's major version number remains unchanged (SemVer guarantees backward compatibility within the same major version). In reality, compatibility is aspirational. Projects often set version numbers without compatibility checks, and even automation can't fully guarantee compatibility.

Incompatible changes slip into minor or patch releases, wreaking havoc on your codebase.

Even nastier are *circular dependencies* (or *cyclic dependencies*), where a library transitively depends on itself (A depends on B, which depends on C, which depends on A, shown in Figure 5-2).

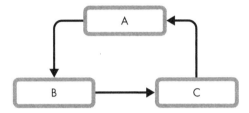

Figure 5-2: *A circular dependency*

Circular dependencies create a chicken and egg problem: upgrading one library breaks the other. Utility or helper projects commonly appear in circular dependencies. For example, a natural language processing (NLP) library depends on a utility library for a string parsing function; unwittingly, another developer adds the NLP library as a utility dependency for a word-stemming utility method.

THE CURIOUS CASE OF GOOGLE COLLECTIONS

Java libraries are packaged into JAR files. During runtime, Java will search all JARs on its classpath to locate classes. This works great until you have multiple JARs that contain different versions of the same class.

LinkedIn had a tool called Azkaban, a workflow engine that let developers upload packages of code and schedule them to run on Hadoop. Azkaban was written in Java and didn't isolate its classpath, meaning all the uploaded code would run with Azkaban's dependencies in addition to their own. One day, jobs began to

(continued)

crash with `NoSuchMethodErrors`. Confusingly, Chris's team could clearly see that the supposedly missing methods existed in the uploaded packages. There was a pattern to the errors: all the missing methods came from the popular Google Guava library.

Guava provides a number of useful features, including making Java's notoriously clunky collection libraries easier to use. The team suspected that there were conflicts between Azkaban's libraries and the packages that were uploaded. It wasn't that simple, though: Azkaban didn't use Guava at all. They eventually realized that Guava had evolved from another library, google-collections, which Azkaban was using. Azkaban pulled in google-collections for two classes, `ImmutableMap` and `ImmutableList`. Java was finding referenced classes in google-collections ahead of Guava and trying to call methods that didn't exist in the earlier version of the library.

The team eventually isolated the classpaths, and Azkaban stopped adding its JARs to the runtime. This mostly fixed the issue, but some jobs continued to fail. They then discovered that packages that were still having problems contained both google-collections and Guava. The build system couldn't tell that google-collections was an older version of Guava, so it included both libraries, causing the same problem as the Azkaban dependency. A lot of careful refactoring had to happen, diverting many engineers from their normal work. Is all of this worth it for some collection helper methods?

Avoiding Dependency Hell

You will absolutely stumble into dependency hell. Dependencies are unavoidable, but every new dependency comes with a cost. Ask yourself if a dependency's value outweighs its cost.

- Do you really need the functionality?

- How well maintained is the dependency?

- How easy would it be for you to fix the dependency if something went wrong?

- How mature is the dependency?

- How frequently does the dependency introduce backward-incompatible changes?

- How well do you, your team, and your organization understand the dependency?

- How easy is it to write the code yourself?

- How is the code licensed?

- What is the ratio of code you use versus code you don't use in the dependency?

When you do decide to add dependencies, use the following best practices.

Isolate Dependencies

You don't have to leave dependency management to build and package systems. Dependent code can also be copied, vendored, or shaded. Copying code into your project trades dependency management automation for more isolation (stability). You'll be able to pick and choose exactly what code you use, but you'll have to manage the code copying.

Many developers are raised on the DRY philosophy, which discourages code duplication. Be pragmatic; don't be afraid to copy code if it helps you avoid a big or unstable dependency (and the software license allows it).

Copying code works best on small, stable code fragments. Manually copying entire libraries has drawbacks: version history can be lost, and you must recopy code every time you update it. *Vendor* code using vendor tools to manage history and updates when embedding entire libraries in your codebase. Vendor folders contain complete library copies. Tools like git-subtree and git-vendor help manage vendor folders in your codebase. Some packaging systems, like Go, even have built-in support for vendor folders.

Dependency *shading* can also isolate dependencies. Shading automatically relocates a dependency into a different namespace to avoid conflicts: some.package.space becomes shaded.some.package.space. This is a friendly way to keep libraries from forcing their dependencies on applications. Shading comes from the Java ecosystem, but the concept applies broadly. Other languages like Rust use similar techniques.

Shading is an advanced technique and should be used sparingly. Never expose a shaded dependency's objects in public APIs; doing so means developers will have to create objects in the shaded package space (shaded.some.package.space.Class). Shading is meant to hide a dependency's existence; creating an object that's been shaded is tricky, and sometimes impossible, for library users. Also, beware that shaded dependencies can confuse developers since package names differ in the build artifact. We recommend only shading dependencies when you are creating a library with widely used dependencies that are likely to create conflicts.

Deliberately Add Dependencies

Explicitly declare as dependencies all libraries you use. Don't use methods and classes from transitive dependencies, even if it seems to work. Libraries are free to change their dependencies even in patch-level version bumps. Your code will stop working if a transitive dependency that you depend on gets dropped during an upgrade.

A project that depends only on the httpclient library (from the earlier example) should not explicitly use classes in httpcore, commons-logging, and commons-codec (httpclient's dependencies); if it does, it should declare a direct dependency on the libraries.

Don't rely solely on the IDE for dependency management. Declare your dependencies explicitly in build files. IDEs often store dependencies in their own project configurations, which build machinery doesn't look at. Inconsistency between your IDE and build files will make code work in the IDE but not when actually building your code, or vice versa.

Pin Versions

Explicitly set every dependency's version number, a practice called *version pinning*. Unpinned versions will be decided by the build or package management system for you. Leaving your fate to the build system is a bad idea. Your code will destabilize when dependency versions change during consecutive builds.

The following code snippet declares a list of Go library dependencies with pinned versions:

```
require (
    github.com/bgentry/speakeasy v0.1.0
    github.com/cockroachdb/datadriven v0.0.0-20190809214429-80d97fb3cbaa
    github.com/coreos/go-semver v0.2.0
    github.com/coreos/go-systemd v0.0.0-20180511133405-39ca1b05acc7
    github.com/coreos/pkg v0.0.0-20160727233714-3ac0863d7acf
    ...
)
```

For contrast, this snippet of Apache Airflow's dependencies uses three different version management strategies:

```
flask_oauth = [
    'Flask-OAuthlib>=0.9.1',
    'oauthlib!=2.0.3,!=2.0.4,!=2.0.5,<3.0.0,>=1.1.2',
    'requests-oauthlib==1.1.0'
]
```

The requests-oauthlib library is explicitly pinned to 1.1.0. The Flask-OAuthlib dependency is set to any version greater than or equal to 0.9.1. And the oauthlib library is extremely specific: 1.1.2 or newer, but not above 3.0.0, but also not 2.0.3, 2.0.4, or 2.0.5. Versions 2.0.3 to 2.0.5 are excluded due to known bugs or incompatibilities.

Bounding the version range is a compromise between an unbounded range and a fully pinned version. The dependency resolution system is free to resolve conflicts and update dependencies, but exposure to breaking changes is limited. But any unpinned versions will pull in more than the latest bug fixes; they'll pull in the latest bugs, behavior, or even incompatible changes.

Even if you pin your direct dependencies, transitive dependencies might still have wildcards. Transitive dependency versions can be pinned by generating a complete manifest of all resolved dependencies and their versions. Dependency manifests go by many names: you freeze requirements in Python, generate *Gemfile.lock*s in Ruby, and create *Cargo.lock*s in Rust. Build systems use manifests to produce identical results on every execution. Manifests are regenerated explicitly by developers when they want to change a version. Committing manifests alongside the rest of your code allows you to explicitly track changes to any of the dependencies, giving you the opportunity to prevent potential problems.

WHY AIRFLOW'S FLASK_OAUTH IS SO MESSY

The elaborate dependency in the previous code block is trying to fix a dependency problem inherited by Airflow from the Flask-OAuthlib library. Flask-OAuthlib had its own unbounded dependencies on oauthlib and requests-oauthlib, which started causing problems. The Flask-OAuthlib developers introduced bounded ranges to their oauthlib and requests-oauthlib dependencies to address this, but it took them a while to release the fix. In the meantime, Airflow broke and couldn't wait for the Flask-OAuthlib release. Airflow copy-pasted the Flask-OAuthlib dependency block as a temporary fix. The change was accompanied by the comment "we can unpin these once a new release of Flask-OAuthlib is released that includes these changes." Eighteen months later, this change has still not been reverted. This is the sort of skulduggery one has to resort to when fixing dependency issues.

Scope Dependencies Narrowly

Dependency scope, discussed earlier, defines when in the build lifecycle a dependency is used. Scoping has a hierarchy: compile-time dependencies are used during runtime, but runtime dependencies are not used to compile code, only to run it. Test dependencies are only pulled in for test execution and are not necessary for normal use of the published code.

Use the narrowest possible scope for each dependency. Declaring all dependencies with compile-time scoping will work but is bad practice. Narrow scoping will help avoid conflicts and reduce runtime binary sizes.

Protect Yourself from Circular Dependencies

Never introduce circular dependencies. Circular dependencies lead to strange build system behavior and deployment ordering problems. Builds will appear to work and then fail suddenly, and applications will have elusive and sporadic bugs.

Protect yourself using build tools. Many build systems have built-in circular dependency detectors that will alert you when a cycle is detected. If your build system doesn't protect against circular dependencies, there are usually plug-ins that can help.

Do's and Don'ts

DO'S	DON'TS
DO use semantic versioning.	DON'T use Git hashes as version numbers.
DO pin dependency version ranges.	DON'T add dependencies unless the value exceeds the cost.
DO use dependency report tools for transitive dependencies.	DON'T use transitive dependencies directly.
DO be skeptical when adding new dependencies.	DON'T introduce circular dependencies.
DO scope your dependencies.	

Level Up

The problem of dependency conflicts and incompatible changes is pervasive; the general term for it is *dependency hell* (and many ecosystems have their own versions—DLL hell, JAR hell, "Any time I have to touch pip"). Though dependency management is complex, there are not many books on the subject; ecosystem-specific discussions and explanations are plentiful online. For a historical perspective, take a look at the Wikipedia article on dependency hell and the references therein.

See *https://semver.org/* for a compact and readable spec on semantic versioning. Python has a similar scheme, defined at *https://www.python .org/dev/peps/pep-0440/*. Both of these versioning schemes are in heavy use and worth learning. There are many others, and it's not uncommon to encounter artifacts using different versioning schemes within the same project. Following the Pareto principle, we don't recommend you dig into version semantics too deep when you are starting out unless it's an explicit part of your job or you need more information to solve a concrete problem. The contents of this chapter should be sufficient for most day-to-day activities.

Many of the versioning concepts in this chapter apply to both libraries and service APIs. We talk more about API versioning in Chapter 11.

TESTING

Writing, running, and fixing tests can feel like busywork. In fact, it's easy for tests to *be* busywork. Bad tests add developer overhead without providing value and can increase test suite instability. This chapter will teach you to test effectively. We'll discuss what tests are used for, different test types, different test tools, how to test responsibly, and how to deal with nondeterminism in tests.

The Many Uses of Tests

Most developers know the fundamental function of tests: tests check that code works. But tests serve other purposes as well. They protect the code from future changes that unintentionally alter its behavior, encourage clean code, force developers to use their own APIs, document how components are to be interacted with, and serve as a playground for experimentation.

Above all, tests verify that software behaves as expected. Unpredictable behavior causes problems for users, developers, and operators. Initially, tests show that code works as specified. Tests then remain to shield existing behavior from new changes. When an old test fails, a decision must be made: Did the developer intend to change behavior, or was a bug introduced?

Test writing also forces developers to think about the interface and implementation of their program. Developers usually first interact with their code in tests. New code will have rough edges; testing exposes clumsy interface design early so it can be corrected. Tests also expose messy implementation. *Spaghetti code*, or code that has too many dependencies, is difficult to test. Writing tests forces developers to keep their code well factored by improving separation of concerns and reducing tight coupling.

Code cleanliness side effects in tests are so strong that *test-driven development (TDD)* has become commonplace. TDD is the practice of writing tests before code. The tests fail when written, and then code is written to make them pass. TDD forces developers to think about behavior, interface design, and integration before cranking out a bunch of code.

Tests serve as a form of documentation, illustrating how the code is meant to be interacted with. They are the first place an experienced programmer starts reading to understand a new codebase. Test suites are a great playground. Developers run tests with debuggers attached to step-through code. As bugs are discovered or questions about behavior arise, new tests can be added to understand them.

Types of Tests

There are dozens of different test types and testing methodologies. Our goal is not to cover the full breadth of this topic but to discuss the most common types—unit, integration, system, performance, and acceptance tests—to give you a firm foundation to build on.

Unit tests verify "units" of code—a single method or behavior. Unit tests should be fast, small, and focused. Speed is important because these tests run frequently—often on developer laptops. Small tests that focus on a single unit of code make it easier to understand what has broken when a test fails.

Integration tests verify that multiple components work together. If you find yourself instantiating multiple objects that interact with each other in a test, you're probably writing an integration test. Integration tests are often slower to execute and require a more elaborate setup than unit tests. Developers run integration tests less frequently, so the feedback loop is longer. These tests can flush out problems that are difficult to identify by testing standalone units individually.

IT'S ONLY OBVIOUS IN RETROSPECT

A few years ago, Dmitriy was shopping for a new dishwasher appliance. He read online reviews, went to a store, dutifully examined all the specs, considered the trade-offs, and finally settled on the model he liked best. The salesperson who insisted on guiding Dmitriy through the aisles checked the inventory, got ready to put in an order, and, just as his hand hovered over the ENTER key, paused. "Is this dishwasher going into a corner in your kitchen, by any chance?" "Why, yes, it is." "And is there a drawer that comes out of a cabinet at a 90-degree angle to where this dishwasher is going, such that it slides into the space right in front of the dishwasher door?" "Why, yes, there is such a drawer." "Ah," the salesperson said, removing his hand from the keyboard. "You will want a different dishwasher." The model Dmitriy selected had a handle that protruded from the door, which would have completely blocked the drawer from coming out. The perfectly functioning dishwasher and the perfectly functioning cabinet were completely incompatible. Clearly, the salesperson had seen this particular integration scenario fail before! (The solution was to purchase a similar model with an inset door handle.)

System tests verify a whole system. End-to-end (e2e, for short) work-flows are run to simulate real user interactions in preproduction environments. Approaches to system test automation vary. Some organizations require that system tests pass before a release, which means all components are tested and released in lockstep. Other organizations ship such large systems that synchronizing releases is not realistic; these organizations often run extensive integration tests and supplement them with continuous synthetic monitoring production tests. *Synthetic monitoring* scripts run in production to simulate user registration, browse for and purchase an item, and so on. Synthetic monitoring requires instrumentation that allows billing, accounting, and other systems to distinguish these production tests from real activity.

Performance tests, such as load and stress tests, measure system performance under different configurations. *Load tests* measure performance under various levels of load: for example, how a system performs when 10, 100, or 1,000 users access it concurrently. *Stress tests* push system load to the point of failure. Stress testing exposes how far a system is capable of going and what happens under excessive load. These tests are useful for capacity planning and defining SLOs.

Acceptance tests are performed by a customer, or their proxy, to validate that the delivered software meets acceptance criteria. These tests are fairly common in enterprise software, where formal acceptance tests and criteria are laid out as part of an expensive contract. The *International Standards Organization (ISO)* requires acceptance tests that validate explicit business requirements as part of their security standard; certification auditors will ask for evidence of documentation for both the requirements and the corresponding tests. Less formal acceptance tests, found in less regulated organizations, are variations on the theme of "I just changed a thing; can you let me know if everything still looks good?"

TESTING IN THE REAL WORLD

We looked at test setups of many successful open source projects while writing this chapter. Many projects were missing certain flavors of tests, while others were inconsistent about the separation— intermingling "unit" and "integration" tests. It's important to know what these categories mean and the trade-offs between them. Still, don't get too wrapped up in getting it perfectly right. Successful projects make real-world pragmatic testing decisions, and so should you. If you see an opportunity to improve the tests and test suites, by all means, do it! Don't get hung up on naming and categorization, and refrain from passing judgment if the setup is not quite right; software entropy is a powerful force (see Chapter 3).

Test Tools

Test tools fall into several categories: test-writing tools, test execution frameworks, and code quality tools. *Test-writing tools* like mocking libraries help you write clean and efficient tests. *Test frameworks* help run tests by modeling a test's lifecycle from setup to teardown. Test frameworks also save test results, integrate with build systems, and provide other helpers. *Code quality tools* are used to analyze code coverage and code complexity, find bugs through static analysis, and check for style errors. Analysis tools are usually set up to run as part of a build or compile step.

Every tool added to your setup comes with baggage. Everyone must understand the tool, along with all of its idiosyncrasies. The tool might depend on many other libraries, which will further increase the complexity of the system. Some tools slow tests down. Therefore, avoid outside tools until you can justify the complexity trade-offs, and make sure your team is bought in.

Mocking Libraries

Mocking libraries are commonly used in unit tests, particularly in object-oriented code. Code often depends on external systems, libraries, or objects. *Mocks* replace external dependencies with stubs that mimic the interface provided by the real system. Mocks implement functionality required for the test by responding to inputs with hard-coded responses.

Eliminating external dependencies keeps unit tests fast and focused. Mocking remote systems allows tests to bypass network calls, simplifying the setup and avoiding slow operations. Mocking methods and objects allows developers to write focused unit tests that exercise just one specific behavior.

Mocks also keep application code from becoming riddled with test-specific methods, parameters, or variables. Test-specific changes are difficult to maintain, make code hard to read, and cause confusing bugs (don't add Boolean isTest parameters to your methods!). Mocks help developers access protected methods and variables without modifying regular code.

While mocking is useful, don't overdo it. Mocks with complex internal logic make your tests brittle and hard to understand. Start with basic inline mocks inside a unit test, and don't write a shared mock class until you begin repeating mocking logic between tests.

An excessive reliance on mocks is a code smell that suggests tight code coupling. Whenever reaching for a mock, consider whether code could be refactored to remove the dependency on the mocked system. Separating computation and data transformation logic from I/O code helps simplify testing and makes the program less brittle.

Test Frameworks

Test frameworks help you write and execute tests. You'll find frameworks that help coordinate and execute unit tests, integration tests, performance tests, and even UI tests. Frameworks do the following:

- Manage test setup and teardown

- Manage test execution and orchestration

- Generate test result reports

- Provide tooling such as extra assertion methods

- Integrate with code coverage tools

Setup and teardown methods allow developers to specify steps, such as data structure setup or file cleanup, that need to be executed before or after each test or set of tests. Many test frameworks give multiple options for setup and teardown execution—before each test, before all tests in a file, or before all tests in a build. Read documentation before using setup and teardown methods to make sure you're using them correctly. Don't expect teardown methods to run in all circumstances. For example, teardown won't occur if a test fails catastrophically, causing the whole test process to exit.

Test frameworks help control the speed and isolation of tests through test orchestration. Tests can be executed serially or in parallel. Serial tests are run one after the next. Running one test at a time is safer because tests have less chance of impacting one another. Parallel execution is faster but more error prone due to shared state, resource, or other contamination.

Frameworks can be configured to start a new process between each test. This further isolates tests, since each test will start fresh. Beware that starting new processes for each test is an expensive operation. See "Determinism in Tests" later in this chapter for more on test isolation.

Test reports help developers debug failed builds. Reports give a detailed readout of which tests passed, failed, or were skipped. When a test fails, reports show which assertion failed. Reports also organize logs and stack traces per test so developers can quickly debug failures. Beware: it's not always obvious where test results are stored—a summary is printed to the console, while the full report is written to disk. Look in test and build directories if you have trouble locating a report.

Code Quality Tools

Take advantage of tools that help you write quality code. Tools that enforce code quality rules are called *linters*. Linters run static analysis and perform style checks. Code quality monitoring tools report metrics such as complexity and test coverage.

Static code analyzers look for common mistakes, like leaving file handles open or using unset variables. Static analyzers are particularly important for dynamic languages like Python and JavaScript, which do not have a compiler to catch syntax errors. Analyzers look for known code smells and highlight questionable code but are not immune to false positives, so you should think critically about problems reported by static analyzers and override false positives with code annotations that tell the analyzer to ignore particular violations.

Code style checkers ensure all source code is formatted the same way: max characters per line, camelCasing versus snake_casing, proper indentation, that sort of thing. A consistent style helps multiple programmers collaborate on a shared codebase. We highly recommend setting up your IDE so that all style rules are automatically applied.

Code complexity tools guard against overly complex logic by calculating *cyclomatic complexity*, or, roughly, the number of paths through your code. The higher your code's complexity, the more difficult it is to test, and the more defects it is likely to contain. Cyclomatic complexity generally increases with the size of the codebase, so a high overall score is not necessarily bad; however, a sudden jump in complexity can be cause for concern, as can individual methods of high complexity.

Code coverage tools measure how many lines of code were exercised by the test suite. If your change lowers code coverage, you should write more tests. Make sure that tests are exercising any new changes that you've made. Aim for reasonable coverage (the rule of thumb is between 65 and 85 percent). Remember that coverage alone isn't a good measure of test quality: it can be quite misleading, both when it is high and when it is low. Checking automatically generated code like scaffolding or serialization

---

classes can create misleadingly low coverage metrics. Conversely, obsessively creating unit tests to get to 100 percent coverage doesn't guarantee that your code will integrate safely.

Engineers have a tendency to fixate on code quality metrics. Just because a tool finds a quality issue doesn't mean that it's actually a problem, nor does it mean that it's worth fixing immediately. Be pragmatic with codebases that fail quality checks. Don't let code get worse, but avoid disruptive stop-the-world cleanup projects. Use Chapter 3's "Technical Debt" section as a guide to determine when to fix code quality issues.

Writing Your Own Tests

You are responsible for making sure your team's code works as expected. Write your own tests; don't expect others to clean up after you. Many companies have formal *quality assurance (QA)* teams with varying responsibilities, including the following:

- Writing black-box or white-box tests
- Writing performance tests
- Performing integration, user acceptance, or system tests
- Providing and maintaining test tools
- Maintaining test environments and infrastructure
- Defining formal test certification and release processes

QA teams can help you verify your code is stable, but never "throw code over the fence" to have them do all of the testing. QA teams don't write unit tests anymore; those days are long gone. If you are in a company with a formal QA team, find out what they are responsible for and how to engage with them. If they're embedded within your team, they are likely attending scrum and sprint planning meetings (see Chapter 12 for more on Agile development). If they're a centralized organization, getting their help might require opening tickets or submitting some formal request.

Write Clean Tests

Write tests with the same care that you write other code. Tests introduce dependencies, require maintenance, and need to be refactored over time. Hacky tests have a high maintenance cost, which slows down future development. Hacky tests are also less stable and less likely to provide reliable results.

Use good programming practices on tests. Document how tests work, how they can be run, and why they were written. Avoid hard-coded values, and don't duplicate code. Use design best practices to maintain a separation of concerns and to keep tests cohesive and decoupled.

Focus on testing fundamental functionality rather than implementation details. This helps when the codebase gets refactored, since tests will still run after the refactoring. If your test code is too tightly coupled with implementation particulars, changes to the main body of code will break tests. These breakages stop meaning something broke, and just signal that the code changed. This does not provide value.

Keep test dependencies separate from your regular code dependencies. If a test requires a library to run, don't force the entire codebase to depend on the library. Most build and packaging systems will allow you to define dependencies specifically for tests; take advantage of this feature.

Don't Overdo Testing

Don't get swept up writing tests. It's easy to lose track of which tests are worth writing. Write tests that fail meaningfully. Avoid chasing higher code coverage just to boost coverage metrics. Testing thin database wrappers, third-party libraries, or basic variable assignments is worthless even if it boosts coverage metrics. Focus on tests that have the largest effect on code risk.

A failing test should tell the developer that something important has changed about the behavior of the program. Tests that fail when trivial changes are made, or when one valid implementation is replaced with another valid implementation, create busywork and desensitize the programmer. One should not need to fix the tests when the code is not broken.

Use code coverage as a guide, not a rule. High code coverage does not guarantee correctness. Exercising code in a test counts toward coverage, but it doesn't mean that it was exercised usefully. It's entirely possible for critical errors to exist in codebases with 100 percent test coverage. Chasing a specific code coverage percentage is myopic.

Don't handcraft tests for autogenerated code such as web framework scaffolding or OpenAPI clients. If your coverage tools aren't configured to ignore generated code, the tools will report the code as untested. Fix the coverage tool configuration in such cases. Code generators are thoroughly tested, so testing generated code is a waste of time (unless you manually introduce changes to generated files, in which case you should test them). If for some reason you discover a real need to test generated code, figure out a way to add tests to the generator.

Focus effort on the highest value tests. Tests take time to write and maintain. Focusing on high-value tests yields the most benefit for the cost. Use a risk matrix to find areas to focus on. A *risk matrix* defines risk as the likelihood and impact of a failure.

Figure 6-1 is a sample risk matrix. The likelihood of a failure is measured on the y-axis, and the impact of the failure is measured on the x-axis. The intersection of the event's likelihood and impact defines its risk.

		Impact			
	Negligible	Minor	Moderate	Significant	Severe
Very Likely	Low Medium	Medium	Medium High	High	High
Likely	Low	Low Medium	Medium	Medium High	High
Possible	Low	Low Medium	Medium	Medium High	Medium High
Unlikely	Low	Low Medium	Low Medium	Medium	Medium High
Very Unlikely	Low	Low	Low Medium	Medium	Medium

Figure 6-1: Risk matrix

Tests shift code risk down the chart—more testing makes failures less likely. Focus on high-likelihood, high-impact areas of the code first. Low-risk or throwaway code, like a proof of concept, isn't worth testing.

Determinism in Tests

Deterministic code always produces the same output for the same input. By contrast, *nondeterministic code* can return different results for the same inputs. A unit test that invokes a call to a remote web service on a network socket is nondeterministic; if the network fails, the test will fail. Nondeterministic tests are a problem that plague many projects. It's important to understand why nondeterministic tests are bad, how to fix them, and how to avoid writing them.

Nondeterministic tests degrade test value. Intermittent test failures (known as *flapping tests*) are hard to reproduce and debug because they don't happen every run, or even every tenth run. You don't know whether the problem is with the test or with your code. Because flapping tests don't provide meaningful information, developers might ignore them and check in broken code as a result.

Intermittently failing tests should be disabled or fixed immediately. Run a flapping test repeatedly in a loop to reproduce the failure. IDEs have features to run tests iteratively, but a loop in a shell also works. Sometimes the nondeterminism is caused by interactions between tests or specific machine configurations—you'll have to experiment. Once you've reproduced the failure, you can fix it by eliminating the nondeterminism or fixing the bug.

Nondeterminism is often introduced by improper handling of sleep, timeouts, and random number generation. Tests that leave side effects or interact with remote systems also cause nondeterminism. Escape nondeterminism by making time and randomness deterministic, cleaning up after tests, and avoiding network calls.

Seed Random Number Generators

Random number generators (RNGs) must be seeded with a value that dictates the random numbers you get from it. By default, random number generators will use the system clock as a seed. System clocks change over time, so two runs of a test with a random number generator will yield different results—nondeterminism.

Seed random number generators with a constant to force them to deterministically generate the same sequence every time they run. Tests with constantly seeded generators will always pass or always fail.

Don't Call Remote Systems in Unit Tests

Remote system calls require network hops, which are unstable. Network calls can time out, which introduces nondeterminism into unit tests. A test might pass hundreds of times and then fail once due to network timeout. Remote systems are also unreliable; they can be shut off, restarted, or frozen. If a remote system is degraded, your test will fail.

Avoiding remote calls (which are slow) also keeps unit tests fast and portable. Speed and portability are critical for unit tests since developers run them frequently and locally on development machines. Unit tests that depend on remote systems aren't portable because a host machine running a test must have access to the remote system, and remote test systems are often in internal integration test environments that aren't easily reachable.

You can eliminate remote system calls in unit tests by using mocks or by refactoring code so remote systems are only required for integration tests.

Inject Clocks

Code that depends on specific intervals of time can cause nondeterminism if not handled correctly. External factors like network latency and CPU speed affect how long operations take, and system clocks progress independently. Code that waits 500 ms for something to happen is brittle. A test will pass if the code runs in 499 ms but fail when it runs in 501 ms. Static system clock methods like now or sleep signal that your code is time dependent. Use injectable clocks rather than static time methods so you can control the timing that your code sees in a test.

The following SimpleThrottler Ruby class illustrates the problem. SimpleThrottler invokes a throttle method when the operation count exceeds a threshold, but the clock is not injectable:

```ruby
class SimpleThrottler
  def initialize(max_per_sec=1000)
    @max_per_sec = max_per_sec
    @last_sec = Time.now.to_i
    @count_this_sec = 0
  end

  def do_work
    @count_this_sec += 1
    # ...
  end

  def maybe_throttle
    if Time.now.to_i == @last_sec and @count_this_sec > @max_per_sec
      throttle()
      @count_this_sec = 0
    end
    @last_sec = Time.now.to_i
  end

  def throttle
    # ...
  end
end
```

In the previous example, we can't guarantee that the maybe_throttle condition will be triggered in a test. Two consecutive operations can take an unbounded amount of time to run if the test machine is degraded or the operating system decides to schedule the test process unfairly. Without control of the clock, it's impossible to test the throttling logic properly.

Instead, make system clocks injectable. Injectable clocks will let you use mocks to precisely control the passage of time in your tests.

```ruby
class SimpleThrottler
  def initialize(max_per_sec=1000, clock=Time)
    @max_per_sec = max_per_sec
    @clock = clock
    @last_sec = clock.now.to_i
    @count_this_sec = 0
  end

  def do_work
    @count_this_sec += 1
    # ...
  end

  def maybe_throttle
    if @clock.now.to_i == @last_sec and @count_this_sec > @max_per_sec
      throttle()
      @count_this_sec = 0
    end
    @last_sec = @clock.now.to_i
  end

  def throttle
    # ...
  end
end
```

This approach, called *dependency injection*, allows tests to override clock behavior by injecting a mock into the clock parameter. The mock can return integers that trigger maybe_throttle. Regular code can default to the regular system clock.

Avoid Sleeps and Timeouts

Developers often use sleep() calls or timeouts when a test requires work in a separate thread, process, or machine to complete before the test can validate its results. The problem with this technique is that it assumes that the other thread of execution will finish in a specific amount of time, which is not something you can rely on. If the language virtual machine or interpreter garbage collects, or the operating system decides to starve the process executing the test, your tests will (sometimes) fail.

Sleeping in tests, or setting long timeouts, also slows down your test execution and therefore your development and debugging process. If you have a test that sleeps for 30 minutes, the fastest your tests will ever execute is 30 minutes. If you have a high (or no) timeout, your tests can get stuck.

If you find yourself tempted to sleep or set a timeout in a test, see if you can restructure the test so that everything will execute deterministically. If not, that's okay, but make an honest effort. Determinism isn't always possible when testing concurrent or asynchronous code.

Close Network Sockets and File Handles

Many tests leak operating system resources because developers assume that tests are short lived and that the operating system will clean everything when the test terminates. However, test execution frameworks often use the same process for multiple tests, which means leaked system resources like network sockets or file handles won't be immediately cleaned.

Leaked resources cause nondeterminism. Operating systems have a cap on the number of sockets and file handles and will begin rejecting new requests when too many resources are leaked. A test that is unable to open new sockets or file handles will fail. Leaked network sockets also break tests that use the same port. Even if tests are run serially, the second will fail to bind to the port since it was opened but not closed previously.

Use standard resource management techniques for narrowly scoped resources, like try-with-resource or with blocks. Resources that are shared among tests should be closed using setup and teardown methods.

Bind to Port Zero

Tests should not bind to a specific network port. Static port binding causes nondeterminism: a test that runs fine on one machine will fail on another if the port is already taken. Binding all tests to the same port is a common practice; these tests will run fine serially but fail when run in parallel. Test failures will be nondeterministic since the ordering of test execution isn't always the same.

Instead, bind network sockets to port zero, which makes the operating system automatically pick an open port. Tests can retrieve the port that was picked and use that value through the remainder of the test.

Generate Unique File and Database Paths

Tests should not write to statically defined locations. Data persistence has the same problem as network port binding. Constant filepaths and database locations cause tests to interfere with each other.

Dynamically generate unique filenames, directory paths, and database or table names. Dynamic IDs let tests run in parallel since they will all read and write to a separate location. Many languages provide utility libraries to generate temporary directories safely (like `tempfile` in Python). Appending UUIDs to file paths or database locations also works.

Isolate and Clean Up Leftover Test State

Tests that don't clean up state cause nondeterminism. State exists anywhere that data persists, usually in memory or on disk. Global variables like counters are common in-memory state, while databases and files are common disk state. A test that inserts a database record and asserts that one row exists will fail if another test has written to the same table. The same test will pass when run alone on a clean database. Leftover state also fills disk space, which destabilizes the test environment.

Integration test environments are complex to set up, so they are often shared. Many tests run in parallel, reading and writing to the same datastores. Be careful in such environments, as sharing resources leads to unexpected test behavior. Tests can affect each other's performance and stability. Shared datastores can cause tests to interfere with each other's data. Follow our guidance in the earlier "Generate Unique File and Database Paths" section to avoid collisions.

You must reset state whether your tests pass or not; don't let failed tests leave debris behind. Use setup and teardown methods to delete test files, clean databases, and reset in-memory test state between each execution. Rebuild environments between test suite runs to rid test machines of leftover state. Tools like containers or machine virtualization make it easy to throw away entire machines and start new ones; however, discarding and starting new virtual machines is slower than running setup and teardown methods, so such tools are best used on large groups of tests.

Don't Depend on Test Order

Tests should not depend on a specific order of execution. Ordering dependencies usually happen when a test writes data and a subsequent test assumes the data is written. This pattern is bad for many reasons:

- If the first test breaks, the second will break, too.

- It's harder to parallelize the tests, since you can't run the second test until the first is done.

- Changes to the first test might accidentally break the second.

- Changes to the test runner might cause your tests to run in a different order.

Use setup and teardown methods to share logic between tests. Provision data for each test in the setup method, and clean up the data in the teardown. Resetting state between each run will keep tests from breaking each other when they mutate the state.

Do's and Don'ts

DO'S	DON'TS
DO use tests to reproduce bugs.	**DON'T** ignore the cost of adding new testing tools.
DO use mocking tools to help write unit tests.	**DON'T** depend on others to write tests for you.
DO use code quality tools to verify coverage, formatting, and complexity.	**DON'T** write tests just to boost code coverage.
DO seed random number generators in tests.	**DON'T** depend solely on code coverage as a measure of quality.
DO close network sockets and file handles in tests.	**DON'T** use avoidable sleeps and timeouts in tests.
DO generate unique filepaths and database IDs in tests.	**DON'T** call remote systems in unit tests.
DO clean up leftover test state between test executions.	**DON'T** depend on test execution order.

Level Up

Many (long) books have been written on software testing. We suggest targeting specific test techniques rather than reading exhaustive test textbooks.

Unit Testing by Vladimir Khorikov (Manning Publications, 2020) is the place to go if you want more on testing best practices. It covers the philosophy of unit testing and common unit test patterns and anti-patterns. Despite its name, the book also touches on integration testing.

Kent Beck's *Test-Driven Development* (Addison-Wesley Professional, 2002) covers TDD in detail. TDD is a great skill to have. If you find yourself in an organization that practices TDD, this book is a must.

Look at the section on property-based testing in *The Pragmatic Programmer* by Andrew Hunt and David Thomas (Addison-Wesley Professional, 1999). We left property-based testing on the cutting-room floor, but if you want to expand your capabilities, property-based testing is a great technique to learn.

Elisabeth Hendrickson's *Explore It!* (Pragmatic Bookshelf, 2013) discusses exploratory testing to learn about code. If you are dealing with complex code, *Explore It!* is a good read.

CODE REVIEWS

Most teams require code changes to be reviewed before they're merged. A culture of high-quality code reviews helps engineers of all experience levels grow and promotes a shared understanding of the codebase. A poor code review culture inhibits innovation, slows down development, and builds resentment.

- - - - - - - - - - - - - -

Your team will expect you to participate in code reviews—both to give and to receive them. Code reviews can bring out impostor syndrome and the Dunning–Kruger effect—phenomena that we discuss in Chapter 2. Both review anxiety and overconfidence are natural, but you can overcome them when armed with the right context and skills.

This chapter explains why code reviews are useful and how to be a good reviewer and reviewee. We'll show you how to get your code reviewed and how to respond when you get feedback. Then, we'll flip roles and show you how to be a good reviewer.

Why Review Code?

A well-executed code review is extremely valuable. There are obvious, superficial benefits—reviews can catch bugs and keep code clean—but a code review's value goes beyond having humans stand in for automated tests and linters. Good reviews act as a teaching tool, spread awareness, document implementation decisions, and provide change records for security and compliance.

Code reviews act as a teaching and learning tool for your team. You can learn from the feedback that your code reviews get. Reviewers will point out useful libraries and coding practices that you might not be aware of. You can also read code review requests from more senior teammates to learn about the codebase and to learn how to write production-grade code (see Chapter 4 for more on writing production code). Code reviews are also an easy way to learn your team's coding style.

Reviewing changes to the codebase ensures that more than one person is familiar with every line of production code. A shared understanding of the codebase helps the team evolve code more cohesively. Having others know what you're changing means you're not the only one the team can go to if things go wrong. On-call engineers will have added context about what code changed when. This shared knowledge means you can take a vacation without worrying about having to support your code.

Records of review comments also serve as documentation, explaining why things were done as they were. It's not always obvious why code is written in a certain way. Code reviews act as an archive for implementation decisions. Having older code reviews to consult provides developers with a written history.

Reviews might even be required for security and compliance purposes. Security and compliance policies often prescribe code reviews as a way to prevent any single developer from maliciously modifying a codebase.

All these benefits of code reviews apply only when all the participants are able to work in a "high trust" environment, in which reviewers are intentional about providing useful feedback and reviewees are open to input. Poorly executed reviews become toxic impediments. Thoughtless feedback provides no value and slows developers down. Slow turnaround time can grind code changes to a halt. Without the right culture, developers can get into knock-down-drag-out disagreements that can ruin a team. Reviews are not an opportunity to prove how smart you are, nor are they a rubber-stamping bureaucratic hurdle.

Getting Your Code Reviewed

Code changes are prepared, submitted, reviewed, and finally approved and merged. Developers start by preparing their code for submission. Once code is ready, they submit the changes, creating a "review request," and reviewers are notified. If there's feedback, back-and-forth discussion occurs, and changes are made. The review is then approved and merged into the codebase.

Prepare Your Review

A well-prepared review request makes it easy for developers to understand what you're doing and provide constructive feedback. Follow the VCS guidance that we give in Chapter 3: keep individual code changes small, separate feature and refactoring work into different reviews, and write descriptive commit messages. Include comments and tests. Don't get attached to the code you submit for review; expect it to change, sometimes significantly, as it goes through the process.

Include a title and description, add reviewers, and link to the issue that your review request is resolving. The title and description are not the same as a commit message. The request's title and description should include added context about how the changes were tested, links to other resources, and callouts on open questions or implementation details. Here's an example:

```
Reviewers: agupta, csmith, jshu, ui-ux
Title: [UI-1343] Fix missing link in menu header
Description:

# Summary
The main menu header is missing a link for the About Us menu option.
Clicking the menu button does nothing right now. Fixed by adding a proper
href.

Added a Selenium test to verify the change.

# Checklist
This PR:

- [x] Adds new tests
- [ ] Modifies public-facing APIs
- [ ] Includes a design document
```

This request example follows several best practices. Both individual reviewers and the entire UI/UX team are added to the review. The title references the issue that's being fixed (UI-1343). Using a standard formatting convention for issue references enables integrations that automatically link issue trackers with code reviews. This is helpful when referring to older issues later.

The description in the review also fills out a code review template that was included with the repository. Some repositories have a description template that gives reviewers important context about the change. A change that modifies a public-facing API might need added scrutiny, for example.

De-risk with Draft Reviews

Many developers think best by coding. Draft changes are a great way to think through and propose a change without investing as much time in writing tests, polishing code, and adding documentation. You can sanity-check what you're doing by submitting a *draft review*: an informal review request intended to get quick and cheap feedback from teammates, which significantly reduces the risk that you go too far down the wrong path.

To avoid confusion, be clear when a code review is a draft or a work-in-progress (WIP). Many teams will have conventions for drafts; usually "DRAFT" or "WIP" is prepended to the title of the code review. Some code review platforms have built-in support for this; for example, GitHub has "draft pull requests." Once your draft feels like it's on the right track, you can transition it out of the "draft" state by finishing the implementation, tests, and documentation, and adding polish. Again, be clear when your code is ready for a nondraft review and then prepare the review request as described in the previous section.

Don't Submit Reviews to Trigger Tests

Large projects often come with complex test tooling. It can be hard, as a new developer, to figure out how to run all relevant tests. Some developers bypass this problem by submitting code reviews to trigger the continuous integration (CI) system. This is a poor practice.

Submitting a code review as a way to trigger test execution is wasteful. Your review will fill the test queue, which will block reviews that actually need their tests to be run before merge. Your teammates might mistake your review request for something they should look at. The CI will run the full test suite, when you might only need to run tests related to your change.

Invest the time to learn how to run your tests locally. Debugging a failed test is easier locally than in CI environments; you won't be able to attach debuggers or get debug information easily on remote machines. Set up your local test environment and learn how to execute just the tests you care about. Make your coding and testing cycle fast so you know immediately if your changes break anything. It's an up-front cost, but it will save you time in the long run (and it's friendlier to your teammates).

Walk Through Large Code Changes

Conduct code walk-throughs when making large changes. Walk-throughs are in-person meetings where a developer shares their screen and walks teammates through the changes that are being made. Walk-throughs are a great way to trigger ideas and get your team comfortable with changes.

Circulate relevant design documents and code in advance, and ask your teammates to take a look before the walk-through meeting. Give them adequate time—don't schedule the walk-through for an hour later.

Start a walk-through by giving background about the change. A quick review of the design document might be warranted. Then, share your screen and navigate the code in your IDE as you narrate. Walk-throughs are best done by navigating through code flow from the start—a page load, API call, or application startup—all the way to the termination of the execution. Explain the main concepts behind any new models or abstractions, how they are meant to be used, and how they fit into the overall application.

Don't try to get your teammates to actually review the code in the walk-through. Attendees should save their comments for the review itself. Walk-throughs are meant to help your team understand why a change is being proposed and to give them a good mental model for working through the code review in detail by themselves.

Don't Get Attached

Getting critical comments on your code can be tough. Keep some emotional distance—the review is of the code, not of you, and it's not even really your code; the whole team will own the code in the future. Getting a lot of suggestions doesn't mean you've failed a test; it means the reviewer is engaging with your code and thinking about how it can be improved. It's completely normal to get lots of comments, particularly if you are one of the less experienced developers on the team.

Reviewers might ask for changes that don't seem important or that seem like they can be addressed later; they might have different priorities and timelines. Do your best to keep an open mind and understand where they are coming from. Be receptive to input and expect to revise your code based on feedback.

Practice Empathy, but Don't Tolerate Rudeness

Everyone communicates differently, but rudeness should not be tolerated. Keep in mind that one person's "short and to the point" can be another's "brusque and rude." Give reviewers the benefit of the doubt, but let them know if their comments seem off base or rude. If a discussion drags on or feels "off," face-to-face discussion can help clear the air and get to a resolution. If you're uncomfortable, talk to your manager.

If you disagree with a suggestion, try to work the disagreement out. Examine your own reaction first. Are you instinctively protecting your code just because you wrote it or because your way is in fact better? Explain your viewpoint clearly. If you still can't agree, ask your manager what the next step is. Teams deal with code review conflicts differently; some defer to the submitter, others to a tech lead, and still others to group quorum. Follow team convention.

Be Proactive

Don't be shy about asking others to review your code. Reviewers are often bombarded with code review and ticket notifications, so reviews can get lost on high-velocity projects. If you don't get any feedback, check in with the team (without being pushy). When you do receive comments, be responsive. You don't want your code review to drag on for weeks. Everyone's memory fades; the faster you respond, the faster you'll get responses.

Merge your changes promptly after you receive approval. Leaving a code review dangling is inconsiderate. Others might be waiting for your changes or want to change code once you merge. If you wait too long, your code will need to be rebased and fixed. In extreme cases, the rebase might break your code's logic, which will require another code review.

Reviewing Code

Good reviewers break a review request into several stages. Triage the request to determine its urgency and complexity, and set aside time to review the change. Begin your review by reading code and asking questions to understand the context of the change. Then, give feedback and drive the review to a conclusion. Combining this recipe with a few best practices will substantially improve your reviews.

Triage Review Requests

Your work as a reviewer begins when you get a review notification. Start by triaging the review request. Some changes are critical and need to be reviewed right away. Most changes, however, are less pressing. If the urgency is unclear, ask the submitter. Change size and complexity also bear consideration. If a change is small and straightforward, a quick review will help unblock your teammate. Larger changes need more time.

High velocity teams can have an overwhelming volume of code reviews. You don't need to review every change. Focus on the changes that you can learn from and those that touch code you are familiar with.

Block Off Time for Reviews

Code reviews are similar to operational work (discussed in Chapter 9); their size and frequency are somewhat unpredictable. Don't drop everything you're doing every time a review request arrives. Left unchecked, review interruptions can torpedo your productivity.

Block off code review time in your calendar. Scheduled review time makes it easy for you to continue on your other tasks, knowing you'll have focused review time later. It'll also keep your reviews high quality—you won't feel as much pressure to get back to other tasks when you have dedicated time.

Large reviews might need additional planning. If you get a review that's going to take more than an hour or two to get through, create an issue to track the review itself. Work with your manager to allocate dedicated time in your sprint planning session (see Chapter 12 on Agile development).

Understand the Change

Don't begin a review by leaving comments; first read and ask questions. Code reviews are most valuable if the reviewer really takes the time to understand the proposed changes. Aim to understand why a change is being made, how code used to behave, and how code behaves after the change. Consider long-term implications of the API design, data structures, and other key decisions.

Understanding the motivation for a change will explain implementation decisions, and you might discover the change isn't even needed. Comparing code before and after the change will also help you check for correctness and trigger alternative implementation ideas.

Give Comprehensive Feedback

Give feedback on a change's correctness, implementation, maintainability, legibility, and security. Point out code that violates style guides, is hard to read, or is confusing. Read tests and look for bugs to verify code correctness.

Ask yourself how you would implement the changes to trigger alternative ideas and discuss the trade-offs. If public APIs are being changed, think about ways this may affect compatibility and the planned rollout of the change (see Chapter 8 to learn more about this topic). Consider ways in which a future programmer might misuse or misunderstand this code and how code can be altered to prevent this.

Think about what libraries and services are available that might help with the changes. Suggest patterns discussed in Chapter 11 to keep code maintainable. Look for OWASP Top Ten (*https://owasp.org/www-project -top-ten/*) violations, like SQL injection attacks, sensitive data leaks, and cross-site scripting vulnerabilities.

Don't be overly terse—write comments the way you would say them if you were reviewing code sitting side by side. Comments should be polite and include both a "what" and a "why":

```
Check that `port` is >= zero and raise an InvalidArgumentException if
not. Ports can't be negative.
```

Acknowledge the Good Stuff

It's natural to focus on finding problems when reviewing code, but a code review doesn't have to be all negative. Comment on the good stuff, too! If you learn something new from reading the code, mention that to the author. If a refactoring cleans up problematic areas of code or new tests feel like they make future changes less risky, recognize these things with a positive, encouraging comment. Even a code change you hate probably has something in it that you can say something nice about—if nothing else, acknowledge the intent and the effort.

> *This is an interesting change. I totally get wanting to migrate the queuing code to a third-party library, but I'm pretty averse to adding a new dependency; the existing code is simple and does what it needs to do. Definitely speak up if I'm misunderstanding the motivation; happy to talk more.*

Distinguish Between Issues, Suggestions, and Nitpicks

Not all review comments have the same level of importance. Major issues need more attention than neutral suggestions and superficial nitpicks.

Don't shy away from stylistic feedback, but make it clear that you're nitpicking. A "nit" prefix prepended to the comment is customary:

```
Nit: Double space.
Nit: Here and throughout, use snake_case for methods and PascalCase for
classes.
Nit: Method name is weird to me. What about maybeRetry(int threshold)?
```

If the same style issue occurs repeatedly, don't keep harping on it; point out the first instance, and indicate that it's something to fix across the board. No one likes to be told the same thing over and over, and it's not necessary.

If you find yourself nitpicking style often, ask whether the project has adequate linting tools set up. Ideally, tooling should do this work for you. If you find that your reviews are mostly nitpicks with few substantial comments, slow down and do a deeper reading. Pointing out useful cosmetic changes is part of a review, but it's not the main goal. See Chapter 3 for more on linting and code-cleanliness tooling.

Call out suggestions that seem better to you but aren't required for approval by prefixing feedback with "optional," "take it or leave it," or "nonblocking." Distinguish suggestions from changes you really want to see made; otherwise, it won't necessarily be clear to the submitter.

Don't Rubber-Stamp Reviews

You're going to feel pressure to approve a review without really looking at it. An urgent change, pressure from a peer, a seemingly trivial change, or a change that's too large will push you to sign off. Empathy might encourage you to turn a review around quickly—you know what it's like to have to wait on a review.

Resist the temptation to rubber-stamp a review with a hasty approval. Rubber-stamping a review is harmful. Teammates will think you know what the change is and why it's applied; you might be held responsible later. The submitter will think you have looked at and approved their work. If you can't prioritize a review adequately, don't review the change at all.

The temptation to rubber-stamp a request might be a signal that the code change is too big for one request. Don't be afraid to ask your teammates to split up large code reviews into smaller sequential chunks. It's easy for developers to get rolling and end up with a multithousand-line change. It's unreasonable to expect a huge code change to be adequately reviewed in one shot. If you feel a code walk-through would be more efficient, you can also ask for that.

Don't Limit Yourself to Web-Based Review Tools

Code reviews are usually handled in a dedicated UI like GitHub's pull request interface. Don't forget that code reviews are just code. You can still check out or download the proposed changes and play with them locally.

A local code checkout will let you examine the proposed changes in your IDE. Large changes are hard to navigate in a web interface. IDEs and desktop-based review tools let you more easily browse the changes.

Local code is also runnable. You can create your own tests to verify things work as expected. A debugger can be attached to running code so you can better understand how things behave. You might even be able to trigger failure scenarios to better illustrate comments in your review.

Don't Forget to Review Tests

Reviewers will often gloss over tests, especially when the change is on the long side. Tests should be reviewed just like the rest of the code. It is often useful to start a review by reading the tests; they illustrate how the code is used and what's expected.

Make sure to check tests for maintainability and code cleanliness. Look for bad test patterns: execution ordering, lack of isolation, and remote system calls. See Chapter 6 for a complete list of testing best practices and violations to look out for.

Drive to a Conclusion

Don't be the reason improvements wither on the vine. Help review submitters get their code approved quickly. Don't insist on perfection, don't expand the scope of the change, clearly describe which comments are critical, and don't let disagreements fester.

Insist on quality, but do not become an impassible barrier. Google's "Engineering Practices Documentation" (*https://google.github.io/eng-practices/*) discusses this tension when reviewing a changelist (CL, Google's internal term for a proposed code change):

> *In general, reviewers should favor approving a CL once it is in a state where it definitely improves the overall code health of the system being worked on, even if the CL isn't perfect.*

Respect the scope of the change that's being made. As you read, you'll find ways to improve adjacent code and have ideas for new features; don't insist that these changes be made as part of the existing review. Open a ticket to improve the code and save the work for later. Keeping scope tight will increase velocity and keep changes incremental.

You can conclude reviews by marking them as "Request Changes" or "Approved." If you leave a lot of comments, a review summary can be helpful. If you're requesting changes, specify which changes are required to meet your approval. Here's an example:

```
Change looks good. Few minor nits, but my main request is to fix the port
handling. The code there looks brittle. See my comment for details.
```

If there is significant disagreement about the code change that you and the author cannot resolve, proactively propose taking the matter to other experts who can help resolve the disagreement.

Do's and Don'ts

DO'S	DON'TS
DO make sure tests and linters pass before requesting a review.	**DON'T** make review requests just to get the CI system to run.
DO set aside time for code reviews and prioritize them just like you do other work.	**DON'T** rubber-stamp code reviews.

(continued)

DO'S	DON'TS
DO speak up if comments seem rude, unconstructive, or inappropriate.	**DON'T** fall in love with your code or take feedback personally.
DO help the reviewer by providing appropriate context for the change.	**DON'T** review code minutiae before understanding the big picture of the change.
DO look beyond superficial style issues when doing a review.	**DON'T** nitpick excessively.
DO use all your tools, not just the code review interface, to understand tricky changes.	**DON'T** let perfect be the enemy of the good.
DO review tests.	

Level Up

Google's "Code Review Developer Guide" at *https://google.github.io/eng-practices/review/* is a good example of a company's code review culture. Keep in mind that the guide is written specifically for Google. Your company's tolerance for risk, investment in automated quality checks, and preference for speed or consistency might lead to a different philosophy.

At the end of the day, code reviews are a specialized form of giving and receiving feedback. The book *Thanks for the Feedback: The Science and Art of Receiving Feedback Well* by Douglas Stone and Sheila Heen (Penguin Books, 2014) is an excellent resource that will help you become both a better reviewer and a better reviewee.

DELIVERING SOFTWARE

You should understand how your code winds up in front of users. Understanding the delivery process will help you troubleshoot problems and control when changes are made. You might not participate in the process directly—it might be automated or performed by release engineers—but the steps between git commit and live traffic should not be a mystery.

- - - - - - - - - - - - - -

Software is delivered when it's running stably in production and customers are using it. Delivery consists of steps such as release, deployment, and rollout. This chapter describes different phases involved in delivering software to customers, source control branching strategies (which affect how software is released), and current best practices.

Software Delivery Phases

Unfortunately, delivery phases do not have industry-standard definitions. Depending on who you talk to, words like *release* and *deploy* can refer to completely different parts of the delivery pipeline. Your team might refer to the whole process, from packaging to rollout, as *releasing*. They might call packaging an artifact a *release*, while making the artifact available for download is *publishing*. They might not say a feature is *released* until it's turned on in production, while everything preceding that action is *deployment*.

For the purposes of this chapter, we refer to four software delivery phases, namely *build*, *release*, *deployment*, and *rollout*, shown in Figure 8-1. Software must first be *built* into packages. Packages should be immutable and versioned. Packages must then be *released*. Release notes and changelogs are updated, and packages are published to a centralized repository. Published release artifacts must be *deployed* to preproduction and production environments. Deployed software is not yet accessible to users—it's just been installed. Once deployed, software is *rolled out* by shifting users to the new software. Once the rollout is complete, software is delivered.

Figure 8-1: Software delivery phases

The delivery process is part of a larger product development cycle. After rollout, feedback is gathered, bugs are detected, and new product requirements are collected. Feature development begins anew, and eventually the next build is kicked off.

Each delivery phase has a set of best practices. These practices will help you deliver software quickly and safely. But before we dive into each delivery step, we need to cover *source control branching strategies*. Branching strategies determine where code changes are committed and how release code is maintained. The right branching strategy will make software delivery easy and predictable, while the wrong strategy will turn delivery into a fight against the process itself.

Branching Strategies

Release packages are built from code in version control systems. *Trunk*—sometimes *main* or *mainline*—contains the main version of a codebase with a history of changes. *Branches* are "cut" from trunk to alter the code; multiple branches allow developers to work in parallel and merge their changes into trunk when ready. Different branching strategies define how long branches should last, how they relate to released versions of the software, and how changes propagate to multiple branches. The two main families of branching strategies are trunk-based and feature branch–based development.

In *trunk-based development*, all developers work off of trunk. Branches are used for a single small feature, bug fix, or update.

Figure 8-2 shows a trunk-based development strategy. A feature branch is created in feature-1 and merged back to trunk. The bug-1 branch is created to fix a bug. A release branch has also been cut, and developers have decided to cherry-pick the bug fix into the 1.0 release.

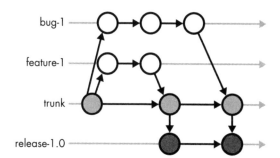

Figure 8-2: *Trunk-based development branches*

Trunk-based development works best when branches are merged back to trunk quickly, in a matter of days if not hours, and not shared between developers. Frequently merging is known as *continuous integration (CI)*. CI reduces risk because changes quickly propagate to all developers, making them less likely to diverge from each other significantly.

Keeping developer codebases in sync prevents potential last-minute integration hurdles and surfaces bugs and incompatibilities early. As a trade-off, bugs in trunk will slow down all developers. To prevent breakages, fast automated tests are run to validate that tests pass before a branch is merged into trunk. Teams often have explicit processes for reacting to a broken trunk; the general expectation is that trunk should always be okay to release, and releases tend to be fairly frequent.

In *feature branch–based development*, many developers simultaneously work on long-lived feature branches, each associated with a feature in the product. Because feature branches are long lived, developers need to *rebase*—to pull in changes from trunk—so the feature branch doesn't diverge too far. Branches are kept stable by controlling when the rebasing occurs. When a release is being prepared, feature branches are pulled into the release branch. Release branches are tested, while feature branches may continue to evolve. Packages are built off stable release branches.

Feature branch–based development is common when trunk is too unstable to release to users and developers want to avoid entering a feature freeze where feature commits are banned while trunk is stabilized. Feature branch–based development is more common in shrink-wrapped software where different customers run different versions; service-oriented systems usually use trunk-based development strategies.

The most popular feature branch approach, described by Vincent Driesen in 2010, is called *Gitflow*. Gitflow uses a develop branch, hotfix branch, and release branch. The develop branch is used as the main branch that feature branches merge and rebase with. Release branches are cut from the develop branch when a release is prepared. Development continues on feature branches during release stabilization. Releases are stabilized and merged into trunk. Trunk is always considered to be production-ready, since it only ever contains stabilized releases. If trunk is unstable because it contains critical bugs, the bugs are addressed immediately with hotfixes instead of waiting for the normal release cadence. Hotfixes are applied to the hotfix branch and merged into both trunk and the develop branch.

The Gitflow example in Figure 8-3 has two feature branches: feature-1 and feature-2. The feature branches are long lived; there are commits and merges back and forth with the develop branch. The release branch has two releases on it, both of which are pulled into trunk. A hotfix branch is used to fix a bug discovered on trunk. This hotfix has also been pulled into the develop branch so feature branches can pull it in.

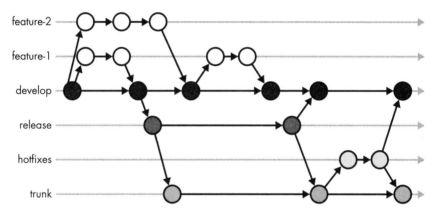

Figure 8-3: *Gitflow feature branch–based development*

Understand and follow your team's branching strategy. Branching strategies define when changes go out, set testing expectations, define your bugfix options, and determine the number of versions your changes must be ported to. Many companies develop internal tools to help manage their VCS workflows. These scripts will branch, merge, and tag for you automatically.

Stick with a trunk-based branching strategy unless you truly need long-lived feature branches. Managing feature branches gets complicated. In fact, Driesen has amended his original Gitflow blog post to discourage Gitflow use for software that can be continuously integrated and delivered.

Build Phase

Software packages must be built before they're delivered. Building software takes many steps: resolving and linking dependencies, running linters, compiling, testing, and, finally, packaging the software. Most build steps are also used during development and have been covered in Chapters 3 to 6. In this section, we'll focus on a build's output: packages.

Packages are built for each release, so software doesn't have to be built on each machine it runs on. Prebuilt packages are more consistent than having each machine compile and run code using its own environment and idiosyncratic combination of tools.

Builds produce multiple packages if the software targets more than one platform or environment. Builds often produce packages for different operating systems, CPU architectures, or language runtimes. You've probably come across Linux package names like this:

- *mysql-server-8.0_8.0.21-1_amd64.deb*

- *mysql-server-8.0_8.0.21-1_arm64.deb*

- *mysql-server-8.0_8.0.21-1_i386.deb*

These MySQL packages were all built for the same MySQL version, but each package is compiled for a different architecture: AMD, ARM, and Intel 386.

Package content and structure varies. Packages can contain binary or source code, dependencies, configurations, release notes, documentation, media, licenses, checksums, and even virtual machine images. Libraries are packaged into language-specific formats such as *JARs*, *wheels*, and *crates*, most of which are just zipped directories arranged to match a spec. Application packages are usually built as zips, tarballs

(*.tar* files), or installation packages (*.dmg* or *setup.exe* files). Container and machine packages allow developers to build not only their software but the environment that it runs in.

Packaging determines what software gets released. Bad packaging makes software difficult to deploy and debug. To avoid headaches, always version packages and split packages by resource type.

Version Packages

Packages should be versioned and assigned a unique identifier. Unique identifiers help operators and developers tie a running application to specific source code, feature sets, and documentation. Without a version, you don't know how a package will behave. If you're unsure what versioning strategy to use, semantic versioning is a safe bet. Most packages follow some form of semantic versioning (see Chapter 5).

Package Different Resources Separately

Software is not just code. Configuration, schemas, images, and language packs (translations) are all part of software. Different resources have different release cadences, different build times, and different testing and verification needs.

Different resources should be packaged separately so they can be modified without having to rebuild the entire software package. Separate packaging lets each resource type have its own release lifecycle and can be rolled forward and backward independently.

If you are shipping a complete application to a customer, the final package is then a meta-package: a package of packages. If you are shipping a web service or a self-upgrading application, you can ship packages separately, allowing configuration and translation to upgrade separately from code.

Python has a long and convoluted package management history, which makes it a great case study. The Python Packaging Authority (PyPA) has published *An Overview of Packaging for Python* (*https://packaging.python.org/overview/*), which attempts to rationalize Python's packaging options. Figures 8-4 and 8-5, created by Mahmoud Hashemi and included in PyPA's overview, show Python's packaging options.

Packaging for Python **tools** and **libraries**

1. **.py** – standalone modules
2. **sdist** – Pure-Python packages
3. **wheel** – Python packages
(With room to spare for static vs. dynamic linking)

Figure 8-4: *Packaging options available to Python tools and libraries*

At the core of the Python library onion is a simple *.py* source file. The next level up, *sdist*, is a group of *.py* files—modules—that are compressed into *.tar.gz* archives. Though sdist packages include all Python code for a module, they don't include compiled code that the package might need. That goes in the next level. In addition to raw Python code, *wheels* include compiled native libraries written in C, C++, Fortran, R, or any other language that the Python package might depend on.

Figure 8-5, which shows application packaging options, is more layered because it includes language runtimes, machine virtualization, and hardware. *PEX packages* include Python code and all of its library dependencies. *Anaconda* provides an ecosystem to manage all installed libraries, not just those your application depends on. *Freezers* bundle not only libraries but also the Python runtime. *Images*, *containers*, and *virtual machines* package operating systems and disk images. In some cases, even *hardware* is a packaging method—shipping embedded systems hardware with application packages, system libraries, and the operating system all installed.

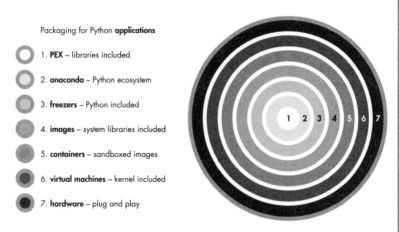

Packaging for Python **applications**

1. **PEX** – libraries included

2. **anaconda** – Python ecosystem

3. **freezers** – Python included

4. **images** – system libraries included

5. **containers** – sandboxed images

6. **virtual machines** – kernel included

7. **hardware** – plug and play

Figure 8-5: Packaging options available to Python applications

While some of these packaging options are Python specific, many languages have similar patterns. Outer layers like machine and container images are language agnostic, and they map to each layer of the packaging stack you use. Understanding your packaging system's assumptions and conventions will prevent deployment issues.

Release Phase

Release publication makes software available to users and enables deployment, the next phase of delivery. Release processes vary based on the type and size of software and user sophistication. An internal web service's release process might be a single step: publishing a software package to a shared package repository. User-facing releases require artifact publication, documentation updates, release notes, and user communication.

Release management is the art of publishing stable, well-documented software at a predictable cadence. Proper release management makes for satisfied customers. Complex software with multiple teams committing to it will often have a release manager role. Release managers coordinate the process—tests, feature validation, security procedures, documentation, and so on.

Understanding release management will help you work with your company's release process effectively. Take ownership of your software's publication by releasing immutable packages frequently. Be clear about release schedules, and publish changelogs and release notes along with new releases.

Don't Throw Releases Over the Fence

Take responsibility for your software's release. Even if your organization has a release engineering or operations team, you should know how and when your software ends up in front of users. Release and operations teams can be of great help in setting up tools, advising on best practices, and automating drudgery and bookkeeping, but they do not know your code as well as you do. Ultimately, it's your responsibility to ensure the software is appropriately deployed and well-functioning.

Make sure your code works in test environments, keep track of release schedules, understand available options, and choose the right approach for your application. If only half of the application ships or a critical bug finds its way to production, you need to be involved in understanding how that happened and how to prevent it from happening again.

Publish Packages to a Release Repository

Release packages are usually published to a package repository or simply tagged and housed in a VCS like Git. Though either practice can work, we encourage you to publish release packages to a purpose-built package repository.

Release repositories serve release artifacts to end users. Docker Hub, GitHub Release Pages, PyPI, and Maven Central are all public repositories.

Many companies also stage releases and publish internal software in private repositories.

Package repositories make release artifacts (another word for a deployable package) available for deployment. Repositories also act as archives—previous release artifacts are accessible for debugging, rollback, and phased deployments. Package contents and metadata are indexed and browsable. Search support makes it easy to find dependencies, version information, and publication dates—invaluable information when troubleshooting. Release repositories are also built to meet deployment demands, handling thousands of users simultaneously downloading a new release.

Version control systems like Git can be used as a release repository, too. Go, for example, uses this approach. Rather than a centralized package repository, Go dependencies are expressed through Git URIs (usually GitHub repositories).

Version control systems work as release repositories, but they aren't built for this purpose. VCSs don't have as many useful search and deployment features. They are not built for large deployments and can get overwhelmed. Production deployments will be impacted if the same VCS machines are handling developer checkouts, tooling requests, and deployment requests. If you find yourself releasing from a VCS, make sure it can handle the load. Sharing one system for both release and development causes operational issues because deployment and development demands are very different. Developers make frequent, small commits and fewer checkouts. Deployments check out code, oftentimes from many machines at once. Deployment demands and developer tools can impact each other's performance if they share the same repository or physical machines.

Keep Releases Immutable

Once published, never change or overwrite a release package. Immutable releases guarantee that all application instances running a specific version will be identical, byte for byte. Identical release packages let developers reason about what code is in an application and how it should behave. Versioned packages that change are no better than unversioned packages.

Release Frequently

Release as frequently as possible. Slow release cycles give a false sense of security: long periods between releases feel like ample time to test changes. In practice, rapid release cycles produce more stable software that is easier to repair when bugs are found. Fewer changes go out per cycle, so each release carries less risk. When a bug makes it to production, there are fewer changes to look at when debugging. Code is fresh in developers' minds, which makes the bug easier and faster to fix.

Software with automated package publication and deployment should be possible to release on every commit. For larger pieces of software that are harder to deploy, balance the frequency of release against the cost of release, deployment, maintenance, and users' rate of adoption.

Be Transparent About Release Schedules

Release schedules define how frequently software is released. Some projects have a predictable time-based schedule, releasing every quarter or year. Other projects release when specific features are completed (milestone-based releases) or simply when they feel like it. Internal systems often publish releases on every commit. Regardless of release style, be clear about release schedules. Publish schedules and notify users when new releases are published.

Publish Changelogs and Release Notes

Changelogs and release notes help your users and your support team understand what is included in a release. *Changelogs* list every ticket that was fixed or commit that was made in a release. To automate changelog

---

creation, track changes in commit messages or issue tracker labels. Release notes are a summary of the new features and bug fixes contained in a release. Changelogs are primarily read by the support and development team, while release notes are for users.

THE APACHE FOUNDATION RELEASE PROCESS

The *Apache Software Foundation (ASF)* provides guidance and resources for open source projects. The ASF release process guidelines are thorough and a great place to look if you want to see a real-world example.

A release manager is nominated to run each ASF project release. Releases include source and often binary packages. Release managers sign artifacts using a cryptographic key so users can verify that downloaded packages came from Apache. Checksums are also included to detect corruption. Releases include LICENSE and NOTICE files to declare various software licenses and copyrights, and all source files include license headers.

Release managers then "cut" a release candidate. Packages are created, and members of a project management committee (PMC) vote to accept or reject the release candidate. PMC members are expected to validate the final artifacts before voting— check that checksums and signatures are valid and that the software passes acceptance tests. Once accepted, artifacts are posted to *https://downloads.apache.org/*. After release, the release manager makes an announcement to Apache project mailing lists and updates the project website with release notes, changelogs, new documentation, and a blog post.

Check out *https://www.apache.org/dev/#releases/* for the complete process, or see Apache Spark's release page for a detailed playbook (*https://spark.apache.org/release-process.html*).

Deployment Phase

Deploying software is the act of getting software packages where they need to be to run. Deployment mechanisms vary—deployment for mobile applications will differ from nuclear reactors—but the same underlying principles apply.

Automate Deployments

Deploy software using scripts rather than manual steps. Automated deployments are more predictable because script behavior is reproducible and version controlled. Operators will be able to reason about deployment behavior when things go wrong.

Scripts are less likely to make mistakes than humans, and they remove the temptation to make manual system tweaks, log in to machines, or manually copy packages during deployment. Mutating state on an existing machine is hard to get right. Two different deployments of the same software can lead to inconsistent behavior that's tough to debug.

Highly evolved automation leads to *continuous delivery*. With continuous delivery, humans are completely removed from deployment. Packaging, testing, release, deployment, and even rollout are all automated. Deployments run as frequently as desired—daily, hourly, or continuously. With continuous delivery, teams can deliver features to their users quickly and get feedback from them. Successful continuous delivery requires a commitment to automated testing (see Chapter 6), automated tooling, and a customer base that is able to absorb rapid changes.

We recommend automating your deployments with off-the-shelf tools. Custom deployment scripts are easy to start with but grow unwieldy fast. Off-the-shelf solutions like Puppet, Salt, Ansible, and Terraform integrate with existing tooling and are purpose-built for deployment automation.

You might find it impossible to fully automate your deployments—that's okay. Deployments that depend on physical actions or third parties are sometimes impossible to fully automate. Just do your best to shrink the boundary of blocking tasks by automating everything around them.

Make Deployments Atomic

Installation scripts often involve multiple steps. Do not assume each step succeeds on every execution. Machines run out of disk, get restarted at the wrong time, or have unexpected file permissions. A partially deployed application can cause future deployments to fail if scripts assume installation locations are empty. To avoid failed partial deployments, make deployment all or nothing (atomic). A partially deployed install should never partially replace the previous successful install, and it should be possible to install the same package to the same machine multiple times, even if previous installation attempts terminated abruptly.

The easiest way to make deployments atomic is by installing software in a different location than the old version; don't overwrite anything. Once packages are installed, a single shortcut or symbolic link can be flipped atomically. Installing packages in a new location has the added benefit that rollbacks become much easier—just point to the old version again. In some cases, different versions of the same software can be run simultaneously on the same machine!

Deploy Applications Independently

Deployment ordering, when one application's deployment requires the upgrade of another application first, is a common problem in software with many applications or services that communicate with each other. Developers ask operations to deploy one application before another or to bring several systems offline to perform the upgrade. Avoid deployment ordering requests. Ordering requirements slow down deployment since applications must wait for each other. Ordering also leads to conflicts where two applications depend on each other to be upgraded.

Build applications that deploy independently. Software that doesn't depend on deployment ordering must be backward and forward compatible. For example, communication protocols must continue to interoperate with newer and older versions. Compatibility is discussed more in Chapter 11.

When a dependency is unavoidable, use the rollout techniques discussed next to safely deploy out of order. Deploying with your changes turned off and turning them on in a specific order later is faster and simpler than enforcing deployment ordering.

DEPLOYMENT BY WIKI

LinkedIn used to release its web services manually. Developers and site reliability engineers attended prerelease meetings to declare which services and configuration changes needed to be deployed, and a large wiki page recorded deployment information.

Release managers would then break the services to be deployed into phases. Developers were not properly managing compatibility, so some services had to be rolled out before others. In some cases, services even called each other, creating a circular dependency. One deployment had more than 20 deployment phases.

On the night of deployment, everyone logged in to an internet relay chat (IRC) channel to monitor the deployment. Site reliability engineers painstakingly copied artifacts to production machines, restarted services, and ran database migration scripts. Step by step, the deployment would go into the early morning hours.

This was a terrible position to be in. Deployments were slow and costly because they had to be done manually. Automation beyond simple scripts was difficult. A failure to deploy one service prevented all downstream services from going out. Developers had to manually verify a deployment before a subsequent phase could progress. Deploys were aggravating, stressful, and tedious.

LinkedIn eventually banned deployment ordering. Services had to support independent deployment or they weren't allowed to ship. The ban created a lot of work—services, tests, tooling, and deployment processes all had to change—but deployments were completely automated. Developers were able to deliver software at their own cadence—multiple times per day if they desired. Site reliability engineers didn't have to babysit deployments, and everyone got more sleep.

Rollout Phase

Once the new code is deployed, you can turn it on (roll it out). Switching everything to the new code at once is risky. No amount of testing will eliminate the potential for bugs, and rolling out code to all users at once can break things for everyone simultaneously. Instead, it's best to roll changes out gradually and monitor health metrics.

There are many rollout strategies: feature flags, circuit breakers, dark launches, canary deployments, and blue-green deployments. *Feature flags* allow you to control what percentage of users receive one code path versus another. *Circuit breakers* automatically switch code paths when there's trouble. *Dark launches, canary deployments,* and *blue-green deployments* let you run multiple deployed versions of your software simultaneously. These patterns mitigate the risk of dangerous changes when used appropriately. Don't go crazy using sophisticated rollout strategies, though—they add operational complexity. Operators and developers must support multiple code versions simultaneously and keep track of which features are toggled on or off. Keep fancy rollout strategies in your toolbox for bigger changes.

Monitor Rollouts

Monitor health metrics such as error rates, response times, and resource consumption as new code is activated. Monitoring can be done manually or automatically. Advanced release pipelines automatically roll a change out to more users or roll the change back based on observed statistics. Even in a fully automated process, humans should keep an eye on the statistics and the rollout progress. More commonly, the decision to ramp up or down is still made by humans looking at logs and metrics.

Determine ahead of time what the general health metrics are. *Service level indicators (SLIs)*, discussed more in Chapter 9, are metrics that indicate the health of your service; watch these for signs of degradation. Think about what you expect to see in metrics or logs that would tell you that your change is functioning correctly. Verify that what you expected to happen is actually happening.

Remember, your job is not done when code is committed, and it's still not done when the code is rolled out. Hold the champagne until metrics and logs are showing your changes running successfully.

Ramp Up with Feature Flags

Feature flags (sometimes called *feature toggles* or *code splits*) allow developers to control when new code is released to users. Code is wrapped in an `if` statement that checks a flag (set by static configuration or from a dynamic service) to determine which branch of code should be run.

Feature flags can be on-off Booleans, allow lists, percentage-based ramps, or even small functions. A Boolean will toggle the feature for all users. Allow lists turn on features for specific users. Percent-based ramps allow developers to slowly turn on the feature for larger swaths of users. It is common to start with company-owned test accounts and then ramp to a single customer before doing an incremental percent-based release. Functions dynamically determine flags based on input parameters, usually passed in at request time.

Feature-flagged code that mutates state needs special attention. Databases are often not controlled by feature flags. New code and old code both interact with the same tables. Your code must be forward and backward compatible. State doesn't go away when a feature is toggled off. If a feature is disabled for a user and then reenabled later, any state changes made while the feature was disabled still exist. Some changes, like database alterations, do not lend themselves to gradual rollouts and must be coordinated with extra care. Isolate feature-flag data if possible, test your code in all flagged states, and write scripts to clean rolled-back feature data.

Make sure to clean up old feature flags that are fully ramped or no longer in use. Code littered with feature flags is difficult to reason about and can even cause bugs; for example, turning off a feature that's been on for a long time can create havoc. Cleaning feature flags takes discipline. Create tickets to remove old flags in the future. Like refactoring, do cleanup incrementally and opportunistically.

Feature flags are sometimes used for *A/B testing*, a technique for measuring user behavior with a new feature. A/B testing with feature flags is fine if users are grouped in a statistically meaningful way. Don't try to A/B test with feature flags unless the flagging system creates test buckets for you, and run your experiment by a data scientist.

Protect Code with Circuit Breakers

Most feature flags are controlled by humans. Circuit breakers are a special kind of feature flag that are controlled by operational events, like a spike in latency or exceptions. Circuit breakers have several unique characteristics: they're binary (on/off), they're permanent, and they're automated.

Circuit breakers are used to protect against performance degradation. If a latency threshold is exceeded, certain features can be automatically disabled or rate limited. Similarly, circuits can break if logs show anomalous behavior—exceptions or a jump in log verbosity.

Circuit breakers also protect against permanent damage. Applications that take irreversible action, such as sending an email or transferring money out of a bank account, use circuit breakers when it's unclear whether to proceed. Databases can also protect themselves by flipping to a read-only mode. Many databases and filesystems will do this automatically if they detect disk corruption.

Ramp Service Versions in Parallel

It is possible to deploy new versions of web services alongside old versions. Packages can be co-located on the same machine or deployed on entirely new hardware. Parallel deployments let you ramp up slowly to mitigate risk and roll back fast if things go wrong. A percentage of incoming service calls are shifted from the old version to a new version using a switch similar to feature flags, but the switch is at the application entry point—usually a load balancer or proxy. Canary deployments and blue-green deployments are the two most common parallel deployment strategies.

Canary deployments are used for services that process a lot of traffic and are deployed to a large number of instances. A new application version is first deployed to a limited set of machines. A small user subset is routed to the canary version. Figure 8-6 shows canary version 1.1 receiving 1 percent of inbound traffic. Like a canary in a coal mine (used to detect the presence of dangerous gases), the canary deployment is an early warning system for new application versions. Malfunctioning canaries impact only a small portion of users, who can be quickly routed back to an old version when errors are encountered.

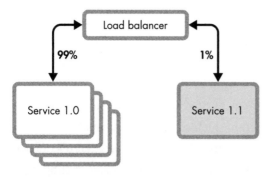

Figure 8-6: In canary deployments, load balancers route a fraction of inbound traffic to a new deployment.

Blue-green deployments run two different versions of the application: one active and one passive. Figure 8-7 shows a passive cluster (called *blue*) running version 1.0 and an active cluster (called *green*) running 1.1. The new version is deployed to the passive environment; when it is ready, traffic is flipped to the new version, and it becomes active, while the previous version becomes passive. Like canaries, if the new version has problems, the traffic can be flipped back. Unlike canaries, traffic is flipped atomically, and the blue and green environments are kept as identical as possible. In a cloud environment, the passive environment is usually destroyed once the release is considered stable.

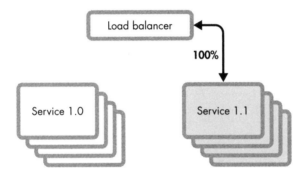

Figure 8-7: *In a blue-green deployment, service 1.0 is kept as a fallback in case service 1.1 malfunctions.*

Blue-green deployments are useful when traffic cannot be easily subset or when running different versions in parallel is not feasible. Unlike canaries, each environment must be able to handle 100 percent of user traffic. In disaster scenarios where all users need to be migrated off a misbehaving system, having the ability to get a parallel environment up and running quickly is invaluable.

Like feature flags, parallel deployments that interact with database and cache state need special care. Both versions of the application must play nicely with each other. Backward and forward compatibility for all schemas must be enforced. This topic is discussed more in Chapter 11.

Launch in Dark Mode

Feature flags, canary deployments, and blue-green releases roll out code to a subset of users and provide mitigation mechanisms when problems arise. Dark launches, sometimes called *traffic shadowing*, expose new code to real-life traffic without making it visible to end users at all. Even if dark code is bad, no user is impacted.

Dark-launched software is still enabled, and the code is invoked, but the results are thrown away. Dark launches help developers and operators learn about their software in production with minimal user impact. Take advantage of dark launches whenever you are releasing particularly complex changes. This pattern is especially useful for validating system migrations.

In a dark launch, an application proxy sits between the live traffic and the application. The proxy duplicates requests to the dark system. Responses to these identical requests from both systems are compared, and differences are recorded. Only the production system's responses are sent to the users. This practice allows the operators to observe their service under real traffic without affecting the customers. The system is said to be in "dark reads" mode when only read traffic is sent to it and no data is modified. A system might be using the same datastore as the production system when operating in dark reads. It is said to be in a "dark writes" mode when writes are also sent to the system and it is using a completely independent datastore. Figure 8-8 shows both modes.

Since operations are happening twice for the same request, once on the production system and once in the dark, you should take care to avoid duplication-related errors. Traffic to the dark system should be excluded from user analytics, and side effects like double billing have to be avoided. Requests can be marked for exclusion by modifying headers to highlight shadowed traffic. Some service meshes, such as Istio, and API gateways, such as Gloo, have built-in support for these operations.

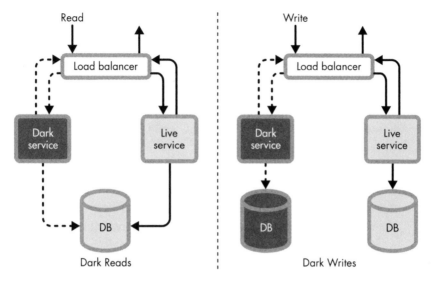

Figure 8-8: *Dark reads and dark writes*

You can do all kinds of cool things with dark launches. The open source tool Diffy, for example, sends dark traffic to three instances of the backend service: two running the production version of the code and one running the new release candidate. Diffy compares responses from a new version and an old version to identify all differences, and compares the responses from the two old versions to identify nondeterministic noise. This allows Diffy to automatically identify expected differences and remove false positives.

WE WANT IT DARKER

Through a series of organizational changes that happened during a rapid growth period, a key service at Twitter fell into disrepair. The service had accumulated a lot of technical debt, but additional feature requests kept coming in. Every change shipped to production was risky—the service was particularly tricky to test, and

(continued)

---

corner cases kept popping up. The engineer who had been toiling away at it all alone was overwhelmed. A lot of their time was spent debugging and fixing production problems. Frequent bugs slowed down the rate at which new changes could go out, which made the feature backlog grow, which increased pressure and made it ever harder to slow down and refactor—all while new features made the codebase more complex.

Eventually, another org change took place, and both the engineer and the service joined Dmitriy's team. After assessing the situation, the team tech lead declared the situation untenable: the team *had* to stop pumping out features and address the technical debt. The engineer maintaining the system had many ideas for improving the service, but even minor changes seemed to trigger unexpected problems in production.

The team decided to focus on production stability first, and they did this with dark writes. They implemented a variant of the Diffy approach—comparing objects in a stream rather than HTTP responses—within two weeks. The service now had a safety net; the team could let a new version "bake" for as long as they wanted, analyzing any unexpected differences in the data it was producing. They could dark launch a change, have user traffic tell them about the edge cases, capture them, add tests and address the problem, and try again.

The test suite grew, the development cycle accelerated, and the team had more confidence in releases. The engineer responsible for the service said it felt like a mountain was lifted off their shoulders. Improvements to the codebase could happen quickly; refactoring it, improving performance, and, yes, even adding new features. It was night and day—and dark writes were what allowed the sun to finally rise.

Do's and Don'ts

DO'S	DON'TS
DO use trunk-based development and continuous integration if possible.	**DON'T** publish unversioned packages.
DO use VCS tools to manage branches.	**DON'T** package configuration, schema, images, and language packs together.
DO work with release and operations teams to create the right processes for your application.	**DON'T** blindly rely on release managers and operations teams.
DO publish release changelogs and release notes.	**DON'T** use VCSs to distribute software.
DO notify users when a release is published.	**DON'T** change release packages once they're published.
DO use off-the-shelf tooling to automate deployment.	**DON'T** roll out without monitoring the results.
DO roll changes out gradually with feature flags.	**DON'T** depend on deployment ordering.
DO use circuit breakers to prevent applications from causing major damage.	
DO use traffic shadowing and dark launches for major changes.	

Level Up

Git for Teams, by Emma Jane Hogbin Westby (O'Reilly Media, 2015), gives more detail on branching strategies. This is a great foundational book and is valuable even if you're not working with Git.

Jez Humble and David Farley's *Continuous Delivery* (Addison-Wesley Professional, 2010) is a deep dive into the topics covered in this chapter. If you spend a lot of time with release engineering, read this book. For a shorter read, Google's *Site Reliability Engineering* (O'Reilly Media, 2016) covers release engineering in Chapter 8.

Michael T. Nygard's *Release It!* (Pragmatic Bookshelf, 2018) is an expansive look at operations topics that our book discusses in Chapters 8 and 9. Nygard's book also spends significant time on software design patterns for operations, a topic we discuss in Chapter 4. We highly recommend *Release It!* for developers working on web services.

Amazon's *Builder's Library* is also a great free resource for delivery best practices. Located at *https://aws.amazon.com/builders-library/*, the library has posts on continuous delivery, automated deployment, and rollbacks.

GOING ON-CALL

M any companies ask engineers to go on-call. On-call engineers are the first line of defense for any unplanned work, be it production issues or ad hoc support requests. Separating deep work from operational work lets the majority of the team focus on development while on-call engineers focus only on unpredictable operational issues and support tasks. Effective on-call engineers are prized by their teammates and managers, and they grow quickly from the relationship-building and learning opportunities that on-call rotations provide.

This chapter covers the basic knowledge and skills you'll need to participate in on-call, incident handling, and support. We'll explain how on-call rotations work and teach you important on-call skills. Then, we'll go in-depth on a real-world incident to give you a practical example of how an incident is handled. After incidents, we'll teach you support best practices. The on-call experience can cause burnout, so we end with a warning about the temptation to be a hero.

If you are in a role where an on-call rotation does not exist, read this chapter anyway. On-call skills apply in any urgent situation.

How On-Call Works

On-call developers rotate based on a schedule. The length of a rotation can be as short as a day, though more often it's a week or two. Every qualified developer takes part in the rotation. Developers who are new to the team or lack necessary skills are often asked to "shadow" a few primary on-call rotations to learn the ropes.

Some schedules have a primary and a secondary on-call developer; the secondary acts as a backup when the primary is unavailable. (Needless to say, developers who routinely cause the secondary on-call to step in are not looked upon kindly.) Some organizations have a tiered response structure: the support team might get alerted first, and then the issue would get escalated to operations engineers, followed by the development team.

Most of an on-call's time is spent fielding ad hoc support requests such as bug reports, questions about how their team's software behaves, and usage questions. On-calls triage these requests and respond to the most urgent.

However, every on-call will eventually be hit with an operational incident (critical problem with production software). An incident is reported to on-call by an alert from an automated monitoring system or by a support engineer who manually observes a problem. On-call developers must triage, mitigate, and resolve incidents.

On-call developers get paged when critical alerts fire. *Paging* is an anachronism from before cell phones—these days, an alert is routed through channels such as chat, email, phone calls, or text messages. Make sure you enter the alerting service's phone number into your contacts if, like us, you don't answer calls from unknown numbers!

All on-call rotations should begin and end with a handoff. The previous on-call developer summarizes any current operational incidents and provides context for any open tasks to the next on-call developer. If you've tracked your work well, handoffs are a nonevent.

Important On-Call Skills

On-call can be a rapid-fire, high-stress experience. Luckily, you can apply a common set of skills to handle both incidents and support requests. You'll need to make yourself available and be on the lookout for incidents. You'll also need to prioritize work so the most critical items get done first. Clear communication will be essential, and you'll need to write down what you're doing as you go. In this section, we'll give you some tips to help you grow these skills.

Make Yourself Available

"Your best ability is availability." This old saying is key to a successful on-call. An on-call's job is to respond to requests and alerts. Don't ignore requests or try to hide. Expect to be interrupted, and accept that you can't do as much deep work while on-call.

Some on-call developers are expected to be near a computer 24/7 (though this doesn't mean staying awake all night waiting for the alerts to fire. It means you're reachable, able to react, and can adjust your non-work plans accordingly). Larger companies have "follow the sun" on-call rotations that shift to developers in different time zones as the day goes on. Figure out what on-call expectations are, and don't get caught in a situation where you can't respond.

Being available does not mean immediately dropping whatever you are doing to address the latest question or problem. For many requests, it's perfectly acceptable to acknowledge that you've received the query and respond with an approximate time when you should be able to look at the problem: "I am currently assisting someone else; can I get back to you in 15 minutes?" A fast response is generally expected from the on-call engineer, but not necessarily a fast resolution.

Pay Attention

Information relevant to on-call work comes in through many channels: chat, email, phone calls, text messages, tickets, logs, metrics, monitoring tools, and even meetings. Pay attention to these channels so you'll have context when debugging and troubleshooting.

Proactively read release notes and chat or email channels that list operational information like software deployments or configuration changes. Keep an eye on chat rooms in which operations teams discuss unusual observations and announce adjustments they are making. Read meeting notes, particularly operational scrum digests that track ongoing incidents and maintenance for the day. Keep operational dashboards up in the background or on a nearby TV so you can establish a baseline for normal behavior. When incidents do occur, you'll be able to tell which graphs look odd.

Create a list of resources that you can rely on in an emergency: direct links to critical dashboards and runbooks for your services, instructions for accessing logs, important chat rooms, and troubleshooting guides. A separate "on-call" bookmark folder that you keep up-to-date will come in handy. Share your list with the team so others can use and improve it.

Prioritize Work

Work on the highest-priority tasks first. As tasks are finished or become blocked, work your way down the list from highest to lowest priority. As you work, alerts will fire, and new questions will come in. Quickly triage the interruption: either set it aside or begin working on it if it's an emergency. If the new request is higher priority than your current task but isn't critical, try to finish your current task, or at least get it to a good stopping point before context switching.

Some support requests are extremely urgent, while others are fine getting done in a week. If you can't tell how urgent a request is, ask what the impact of the request is. The impact will determine the priority. If you disagree with the requestor about an issue's prioritization, discuss it with your manager.

On-call work is categorized by priority: P0, P1, P2, and so on. Prioritizing work into categories helps define a task's urgency. Category names and meaning vary by company, but P0 tasks are the big ones. Google Cloud's support priority ladder offers one example of how priority levels may be defined (*https://cloud.google.com/support/docs/best-practice #setting_the_priority_and_escalating/*):

- P1: Critical Impact—Service Unusable in Production

- P2: High Impact—Service Use Severely Impaired

- P3: Medium Impact—Service Use Partially Impaired

- P4: Low Impact—Service Fully Usable

Service level indicators, objectives, and agreements also help prioritize operational work. *Service level indicators (SLIs)* such as error rate, request latency, and requests per second are the easiest way to see if an application is healthy. *Service level objectives (SLOs)* define SLI targets for healthy application behavior. If error rate is an SLI for an application, an SLO might be a request error rate less than 0.001 percent. *Service level agreements (SLAs)* are agreements about what happens when an SLO is missed. (Companies that violate SLAs with their customers usually need to return money and may even face contract termination.) Learn the SLIs, SLOs, and SLAs for your applications. SLIs will point you to the most important metrics. SLOs and SLAs will help you prioritize incidents.

Communicate Clearly

Clear communication is critical when dealing with operational tasks. Things happen quickly, and miscommunication can cause major problems. To communicate clearly, be polite, direct, responsive, and thorough.

Under a barrage of operational tasks and interruptions, developers get stressed and grumpy—it's human nature. Be patient and polite when responding to support tasks. While it might be your 10th interruption of the day, it's the requestor's first interaction with you.

Communicate in concise sentences. It can feel uncomfortable to be direct, but being direct doesn't mean being rude. Brevity ensures that your communication is read and understood. If you don't know an answer, say so. If you do know the answer, speak up.

Respond to requests quickly. Responses don't have to be solutions. Tell the requestor that you've seen their request, and make sure you understand the problem:

> *Thanks for reaching out. To clarify: the login service is getting 503 response codes from the profile service? You're not talking about auth, right? They're two separate services, but confusingly named.*

Post status updates periodically. Updates should include what you've found since your last update and what you're planning on doing next. Every time you make an update, provide a new time estimate:

> *I looked at the login service. I don't see a spike in error rate, but I'll take a look at the logs and get back to you. Expect an update in an hour.*

Track Your Work

Write down what you're doing as you work. Each item that you work on while on-call should be in an issue tracker or the team's on-call log. Track progress as you work by writing updates in each ticket. Include the final steps that mitigated or resolved the issue in the ticket so you'll have the solution documented if the issue appears again. Tracking progress reminds you where you left off when you come back to a ticket after an interruption. The next on-call will be able to see the state of ongoing work by reading your issues, and anyone you ask for help can read the log to catch up. Logged questions and incidents also create a searchable knowledge base that future on-calls can refer to.

Some companies use chat channels like Slack for operational incidents and support. Chat is a good way to communicate, but chat transcripts are hard to read later, so make sure to summarize everything in a ticket or document. Don't be afraid to redirect support requests to appropriate channels. Be direct: "I'll start looking into this right now. Could you open a ticket so this is counted when we evaluate our support workload?"

Close finished issues so dangling tickets don't clutter on-call boards and skew on-call support metrics. Ask the requestor to confirm that their issue has been addressed before closing their ticket. If a requestor isn't responding, say that you're going to close the ticket in 24 hours due to lack of response; then do so.

Always include timestamps in your notes. Timestamps help operators correlate events across the system when debugging issues. Knowing that a service was restarted at 1 PM is useful when customers begin reporting latency at 1:05 PM.

Handling Incidents

Incident handling is an on-call's most important responsibility. Most developers think handling an incident is about fixing a production problem. Resolving the problem is important, but in a critical incident, the top objective is to mitigate the impact of the problem and restore service. The second objective is to capture information to later analyze how and why the problem happened. Determining the cause of the incident, proving it to be the culprit, and fixing the underlying problem is only your *third* priority.

Incident response is broken into these five steps:

1. **Triage**: Engineers must find the problem, decide its severity, and determine who can fix it.

2. **Coordination**: Teams (and potentially customers) must be notified of the issue. If the on-call can't fix the problem themselves, they must alert those who can.

3. **Mitigation**: Engineers must get things stable as quickly as possible. Mitigation is not a long-term fix; you are just trying to

"stop the bleeding." Problems can be mitigated by rolling back a release, failing over to another environment, turning off misbehaving features, or adding hardware resources.

4. **Resolution**: After the problem is mitigated, engineers have some time to breathe, think, and work toward a resolution. Engineers continue to investigate the problem to determine and address underlying issues. The incident is resolved once the immediate problem has been fixed.

5. **Follow-up**: An investigation is conducted into the root cause— why it happened in the first place. If the incident was severe, a formal postmortem, or retrospective, is conducted. Follow-up tasks are created to prevent the root cause (or causes) from happening again. Teams look for any gaps in process, tooling, or documentation. The incident is not considered done until all follow-up tasks have been completed.

The phases of an incident can sound abstract. To make things clear, we'll walk you through a real incident and point out the different phases as we go. The incident occurs when data fails to load into a data warehouse. *Data warehouses* are databases meant to serve analytical queries for reports and machine learning. This particular data warehouse is kept up-to-date by a stream of updates in a real-time messaging system. Connectors read messages from the streaming system and write them into the warehouse. The data in the data warehouse is used by teams across the company for both internal and customer-facing reports, machine learning, application debugging, and more.

Triage

Determine a problem's priority by looking at its impact: How many people is it affecting, and how detrimental is it? Use your company's prioritization categories and SLO/SLA definitions to prioritize the issue, with the help of SLIs and the metric that triggered the alert, if applicable.

REAL-WORLD EXAMPLE

The operations team gets paged when monitors detect data in the messaging system that isn't in the data warehouse. The incident triggers the first on-call step: *triage* (acknowledging the issue and understanding its impact so it can be prioritized properly). The on-call engineer acknowledges the page and begins investigating the problem to determine the priority. Since the alert shows data is missing in tables used to generate customer reports, they deem the issue high priority.

The triage phase has now ended. The engineer acknowledged the alert and determined the priority but did not try to solve the problem; they simply looked to see which tables were impacted.

If you're having trouble determining issue severity, ask for help. Triage is not the time to prove you can figure things out on your own; time is of the essence.

Likewise, triage is not the time to troubleshoot problems. Your users will continue to suffer while you troubleshoot. Save troubleshooting for the mitigation and resolution phases.

Coordination

REAL-WORLD EXAMPLE

At this point, the on-call engineer switches into *coordination* mode. They post an announcement in the operations chat channel stating that they are seeing a gap in data for customer-facing tables. A cursory investigation shows that the connector that loads data into the data warehouse is running, and the logs don't indicate any faults.

(continued)

> The on-call engineer asks for help from some of the connector developers and pulls in another engineer with connector experience. The engineering manager that the on-call engineer reports to steps in to act as the incident manager. The team sends out an email to the company notifying everyone that data is missing from the warehouse for several tables. The incident manager works with account management and operations to post a notice on the customer-facing status page.

Coordination starts by figuring out who's in charge. For lower-priority incidents, the on-call is in charge and will coordinate. For larger incidents, an *incident commander* will take charge. Commanders keep track of who is doing what and what the current state of the investigation is.

Once someone takes charge, all relevant parties must be notified of the incident. Contact everyone needed to mitigate or resolve the problem—other developers or SREs. Internal stakeholders such as technical account managers, product managers, and support specialists might need to be notified. Impacted users might need to be alerted through status pages, emails, Twitter alerts, and so on.

Many different conversations will happen in parallel, which makes it difficult to follow what's happening. Large incidents have war rooms to help with communication. *War rooms* are virtual or physical spaces used to coordinate incident response. All interested parties join the war room to coordinate response.

Track communication in written form in a central location: a ticketing system or chat. Communicating helps everyone track progress, saves you from constantly answering status questions, prevents duplicate work, and enables others to provide helpful suggestions. Share both your observations and your actions, and state what you are about to do before you do it. Communicate your work even if you are working alone—someone might join later and find the log helpful, and a detailed record will help to reconstruct the timeline afterward.

Mitigation

REAL-WORLD EXAMPLE

While notifications are sent, the engineers move on to *mitigation*. The decision is made to bounce (restart) the connector to see if it becomes unwedged (unstuck), but the issue remains. A stack dump shows the connector reading and deserializing (decoding) messages. The machine running the connector has a completely saturated CPU (100 percent usage), so the engineers guess that the connector is getting stuck on a large or corrupt message that is causing it to chew up all of the CPU during deserialization.

The engineers decide to try to mitigate the problem by running a second connector with just the known good streams. There are 30 streams, and the engineers don't know which streams have bad messages. They decide to binary search to find the corrupt streams: half are added, and then the set is adjusted based on the connector's behavior. Eventually, the team finds the stream that is causing the problem. The connector is restarted with all the healthy streams, and their table data catches up. The impact of the problem is now limited to a single stream and table.

Your goal in the mitigation phase is to reduce the problem's impact. Mitigation isn't about fixing the problem; it's about reducing its severity. Fixing a problem can take a lot of time, while mitigating it can usually be done quickly.

Incidents are commonly mitigated by rolling back a software release to a "last known good" version or by shifting traffic away from the problem. Depending on the situation, mitigation might involve turning off a feature flag, removing a machine from a pool, or rolling back a just-deployed service.

Ideally, the software you're working with will have a runbook for the problem. *Runbooks* are predefined step-by-step instructions to mitigate common problems and perform actions such as restarts and rollbacks. Make sure you know where runbooks and troubleshooting guides can be found.

Capture what data you can as you work to mitigate the problem. Once mitigated, the problem might be hard to reproduce. Quickly saving telemetry data, stack traces, heap dumps, logs, and screenshots of dashboards will help with debugging and root-cause analysis later.

You'll often find gaps in metrics, tooling, and configuration while trying to mitigate the problem. Important metrics might be missing, incorrect permissions might be granted, or systems might be misconfigured. Quickly write down any gaps that you find—anything that would have made your life better while troubleshooting. Open tickets during the follow-up phase to address these gaps.

Resolution

REAL-WORLD EXAMPLE

The engineers now drive to a *resolution*. One stream appears to have a bad message, and the data warehouse table for this stream still isn't getting data.

Engineers remove all healthy streams from the original connector to try to reproduce the issue. The team can now see the message that the connector is stuck on, so they manually read the message using a command line tool. Everything looks fine.

At this point, the team has an epiphany—how is it that the command line tool can read the message but the connector can't? It appears that the connector includes some code that isn't used in the command line tool—a fancy date deserializer. The date deserializer infers a message header's data type (integer, string, date, and so on) using complicated logic. The command line tool doesn't print message headers by default. Engineers rerun the tool with message headers enabled and discover that the bad message has a header with a single key but an empty value.

The header's key hints that the message header is injected by an *application performance management (APM)* tool. APMs sit inside applications and tell developers about the behavior of a running application: memory usage, CPU usage, and stack traces. Unbeknownst to the engineers, the APM daemon is injecting headers into all messages.

The team contacts outside support. Support engineers for the streaming system tell the engineers that the command line tool has a bug: it won't print message headers that contain a null-terminated byte string. The engineers believe there are bytes in headers that are causing the type inference to get stuck.

The team disables header decoding in the connector to test the theory. Data for the last remaining table quickly loads into the data warehouse. All tables are now up-to-date, and the monitors begin to pass their data quality checks. The team notifies the support channel of the resolution and updates the customer-facing status page.

Once mitigation is complete, the incident is no longer an emergency. You can take time to troubleshoot and resolve the underlying issues. In our example incident, the priority was dropped once the customer-facing streams recovered. This gave breathing room to the engineers so they could investigate the problem.

During the resolution phase, focus on the immediate technical problems. Focus on what is needed to recover without the temporary measures put in place during mitigation. Set aside larger technical and process problems for the follow-up phase.

Use the scientific method to troubleshoot technical problems. Chapter 12 of Google's *Site Reliability Engineering* book offers a *hypothetico-deductive* model of the scientific method. Examine the problem, make a diagnosis, and then test and treat. If the treatment is successful, the problem is cured; if not, you reexamine and start again. The team in our example applied the scientific method when they formed a hypothesis that the connector was having deserialization issues and not dropping data. They looked at metric data and did their binary-search experiment to find the bad stream. If they came up empty-handed, the team would need to reformulate a new hypothesis.

Ideally, you can quarantine a misbehaving program instance and examine its misbehavior. The engineers in our connector example did this when they isolated the bad stream to a separate connector. Your goal during resolution is to understand the symptoms of the problem and try to make it reproducible. Use all the operational data at your disposal: metrics, logs, stack traces, heap dumps, change notifications, issue tickets, and communications channels.

Once you have a clear view of the symptoms, diagnose the problem by looking for the causes. Diagnosis is a search, and like any search, you can use search algorithms to troubleshoot. For small problems, a linear search—examining components front to back—is fine. Use divide and conquer or a binary search (also called *half-splitting*) on bigger systems. Find a point halfway through the call stack and see if the problem is upstream or downstream of the issue. If the problem is upstream, pick a new component halfway upstream; if it's downstream, do the reverse. Keep iterating until you find the component where you believe the problem is occurring.

Next, test your theory. Testing isn't treatment—you're not fixing the problem yet. Instead, see if you can control the bad behavior. Can you reproduce it? Can you change a configuration to make the problem go away? If so, you've located the cause. If not, you've eliminated one potential cause—go back, reexamine, and formulate a new diagnosis to test.

Once the team in the connector example believed they had narrowed the problem to a header deserialization issue, they tested their theory by disabling header decoding in the connector configuration.

After a successful test, you can decide on the best course of treatment. Perhaps a configuration change is all that's needed. Often, a bug fix will need to be written, tested, and applied. Apply the treatment and verify that it's working as expected. Keep an eye on metrics and logs until you're convinced everything is stable.

Follow-Up

> ### REAL-WORLD EXAMPLE
>
> The engineering manager responsible for the connector schedules *follow-up* work, and the on-call engineer writes a postmortem draft document. A postmortem meeting is scheduled. Eventually, through the postmortem process, tickets are opened to investigate why the APM was using message headers, why the connect consumer couldn't deserialize them, and why the manual consumer couldn't print headers with null strings.

Incidents are a big deal, so they need follow-up. The goal is to learn from the incident and to prevent it from happening again. A *postmortem* document is written and reviewed, and tasks are opened to prevent recurrence.

Note *The term* postmortem *is borrowed from the medical field, where an* after-death *examination is conducted and written up when a patient dies. Fortunately, in our case, stakes are less dire. A perfectly acceptable alternative term is* retrospective, *which has the added benefit of being the term we use for other after-the-fact discussions, like the sprint retrospectives we discuss in Chapter 12.*

The on-call engineer who dealt with the incident is responsible for drafting a postmortem document, which should capture what happened, what was learned, and what needs to be done to prevent the incident from happening again. There are many approaches and templates for writing a postmortem. One good example is Atlassian's postmortem template (*https://www.atlassian.com/incident-management/postmortem/templates/*). The template has sections and examples describing the lead-up, fault, impact, detection, response, recovery, timeline, root cause, lessons learned, and corrective actions needed.

A critical section of any postmortem document is the *root-cause analysis (RCA)* section. Root-cause analysis is performed using the five whys. This technique is pretty simple: keep asking why. Take a problem and ask why it happened. When you get an answer, ask why again. Keep asking why until you get to the root cause. The "five" is anecdotal—most problems take about five iterations to get to the root cause.

PROBLEM: DATA MISSING FROM DATA WAREHOUSE

1. **Why?** The connector wasn't loading data into the data warehouse.

2. **Why?** The connector couldn't deserialize incoming messages.

3. **Why?** The incoming messages had bad headers.

4. **Why?** The APM was inserting headers into the messages.

5. **Why?** The APM defaulted to this behavior without developer knowledge.

In this example, the root cause was the APM's accidental message header configuration.

Note *Root-cause analysis is a popular but misleading term. Incidents are rarely caused by a single issue. In practice, the five whys might lead to many different causes. This is fine; just document everything.*

After a postmortem document is written, one of the managers or tech leads schedules a review meeting with all interested parties. The postmortem document author leads the review, and participants discuss each section in detail. The author adds missing information and new tasks as they're discovered during discussion.

It's easy to get upset and cast blame in high-stress situations. Do your best to provide constructive feedback. Point out areas for improvement, but avoid blaming individuals or teams for problems. "Peter didn't disable message headers" assigns blame, while "Message header config changes aren't going through code review" is an area for improvement. Don't let postmortems turn into unhealthy vent fests.

Good postmortem meetings also keep "solutioning" separate from the review meeting. *Solutioning*—figuring out how to solve a problem—takes a long time and distracts from the purpose of the meeting: to discuss problems and assign tasks. "The message had a bad header" is a problem, while "We should put bad messages in a dead letter queue" is a solution. Any solutioning should happen in follow-up tasks.

After a postmortem meeting, follow-up tasks must be completed. If tasks are assigned to you, work with your manager and the postmortem team to prioritize them properly. An incident can't be closed until all remaining follow-up tasks have been finished.

Old postmortem documents are a great way to learn. Some companies even share their postmortem documents publicly as valuable resources for the whole community to learn from. Look at Dan Luu's collection for inspiration (*https://github.com/danluu/post-mortems*). You might find postmortem reading groups at your company, too. Teams get together to review postmortem documents with a wider audience. Some teams even use old postmortem documents to simulate production issues to train new engineers.

Providing Support

When on-call engineers aren't dealing with incidents, they spend time handling support requests. These requests come both from within the organization and from external customers, and they run the gamut from simple "Hey, how does this work?" questions to difficult troubleshooting problems. Most requests are bug reports, questions about business logic, or technical questions about how to use your software.

Support requests follow a pretty standard flow. When a request comes in, you should acknowledge that you've seen it and ask questions to make sure you understand the problem. Once you've got a grasp on the problem, give a time estimate on the next update: "I'll get back to you by 5 PM with an update." Next, start investigating, and update the requestor as you go. Follow the same mitigation and resolution strategies that we outlined earlier. When you think the issue is resolved, ask the requestor to confirm. Finally, close out the request. Here's an example:

> *[3:48 PM] Sumeet: I'm getting reports from customers saying page loads are slow.*
>
> *[4:12 PM] Janet: Hi, Sumeet. Thanks for reporting this. Can I get a few more pieces of information? Can you give me one or two customer IDs that reported slowness and any particular pages they are seeing the issue on? Our dashboards aren't showing any widespread latency.*
>
> *[5:15 PM] Sumeet: Customer IDs 1934 and 12305. Pages: the ops main page (/ops) and the APM chart (/ops/apm/dashboard). They're saying loads are taking > 5 seconds.*
>
> *[5:32 PM] Janet: Great, thanks. I'll have an update for you by 10 tomorrow morning.*
>
> *[8:15 AM] Janet: Okay, I think I know what's going on. We had maintenance on the database that powers the APM dashboard yesterday afternoon. It impacted the ops main page since we show a roll-up there,*

too. The maintenance finished around 8 PM. Can you confirm that the customer is no longer seeing the issue?

[9:34 AM] Sumeet: Awesome! Just confirmed with a couple of the customers who reported the issue. Page loads are now much better.

This example illustrates many practices covered in "Important On-Call Skills." Janet, the on-call, is *paying attention* and *makes herself available*; she responds within a half hour of the first request. Janet *communicates clearly* by asking clarifying questions to understand the problem and its impact so she can properly *prioritize the issue*. She posts an ETA for the next update when she has enough information to investigate. Once Janet believes the problem is solved, she *tracks her work* by describing what happened and asks the requestor to confirm it's not an issue anymore.

Support can feel like a distraction, since your "real" job is programming. Think of support as an opportunity to learn. You'll get to see how your team's software is used in the real world and the ways in which it fails or confuses users. Answering support requests will take you to parts of the code you were not familiar with; you'll have to think hard and experiment. You will notice patterns that cause problems, which will help you create better software in the future. Support rotations will make you a better engineer. Plus, you get to help others and build relationships and your reputation. Fast, high-quality support responses do not go unnoticed.

Don't Be a Hero

We've spent quite a few words in this chapter encouraging you not to shy away from on-call responsibilities and ad hoc support requests. There is another extreme we want to warn you about: doing too much. On-call activities can feel gratifying. Colleagues routinely thank you for helping them with issues, and managers praise efficient incident resolution. However, doing too much can lead to burnout.

For some engineers, jumping into "firefighting" mode becomes a reflex as they become more experienced. Talented firefighting engineers can be a godsend to a team: everyone knows that when things get tough, all they need to do is ask the firefighter, and they'll fix it. Depending on a firefighter is not healthy. Firefighters who are pulled into every issue effectively become permanently on-call. The long hours and high stakes will cause burnout. Firefighter engineers also struggle with their programming or design work because they are constantly being interrupted. And teams that rely on a firefighter won't develop their own expertise and troubleshooting abilities. Firefighter heroics can also cause fixes for serious underlying problems to be deprioritized because the firefighter is always around to patch things up.

If you feel that you are the only one who can fix a problem or that you are routinely involved in firefighting when not on-call, you might be becoming a "hero." Talk to your manager or tech lead about ways to find better balance and get more people trained and available to step in. If there's a hero on your team, see if you can learn from them and pick up some of the burden; let them know when you are okay struggling a bit: "Thanks, Jen. I actually want to try to figure this out on my own for a bit so I can skill up . . . Can I ask for your help in 30 minutes if this is still a mystery?"

Do's and Don'ts

DO'S	DON'TS
DO add known "pager" numbers to your phone's contacts.	**DON'T** ignore alerts.
DO use priority categories, SLIs, SLOs, and SLAs to prioritize incident response.	**DON'T** try to troubleshoot during triage.

DO'S	DON'TS
DO triage, coordinate, mitigate, resolve, and follow up on critical incidents.	**DON'T** leave a problem unmitigated while you search for the root cause.
DO use the scientific method to troubleshoot.	**DON'T** cast blame during postmortems.
DO ask "the five whys" when following up on an incident.	**DON'T** hesitate to close nonresponsive support requests.
DO acknowledge support requests.	**DON'T** ask support requestors what their priority is; ask about the impact of the problem.
DO give time estimates and periodic updates.	**DON'T** be a hero who has to fix all the things.
DO confirm a problem is fixed before closing a support request ticket.	
DO redirect support requests to the appropriate communication channels.	

Level Up

The five phases of incident response in our "Handling Incidents" section come from an *Increment* article, "What Happens When the Pager Goes Off?" (*https://increment.com/on-call/when-the-pager-goes-off/*). The article has more quotes and detail around how different companies handle incidents.

In more nascent operations settings, developers might need to define SLIs and SLOs themselves. If you find yourself responsible for SLIs and SLOs, we highly recommend Chapter 4 of Google's *Site Reliability Engineering* book.

Chapters 11, 13, 14, and 15 of *Site Reliability Engineering* cover on-call, emergency response, incident handling, and postmortems. We've included the most important information for new engineers in our chapter, but Google's book provides more detail if you want to go deeper.

TECHNICAL DESIGN PROCESS

W hen asked to make a change, most entry-level engineers jump straight into coding. Diving into code works at first, but you'll eventually be given a task that's too big to jump into; you'll need to think about technical design.

The *technical design process* helps everyone agree on a design for a large change. Design work is broken into two activities: solitary deep-thought work and collaborative group discussion. Researching, brain-storming, and writing make up the deep work. Design discussions and commenting on design documents make up the collaborative part. The tangible output of the process is a design document.

This chapter describes an expansive version of the design process, suitable for large changes. The process can look slow and intimidating. Some engineers are traumatized by heavyweight design processes gone awry. It's okay to scale things down for smaller changes. The problem you're solving might be captured in three sentences, not a paragraphs-long essay. Design template sections might be irrelevant, multiple rounds of feedback might be unnecessary, and a review from other teams might not be needed. You will develop a feel for the right amount of input and collaboration for a problem. In the beginning, err on the side of caution: ask your tech lead or manager for guidance, and share your design widely. Done correctly, participating in and leading technical design work is rewarding and valuable.

The Technical Design Process Cone

Designing software is not a linear process from research and brainstorming to documentation and approval. It is more like a spiral that alternates between independent and collaborative work, clarifying and refining the design at every step (see Figure 10-1).

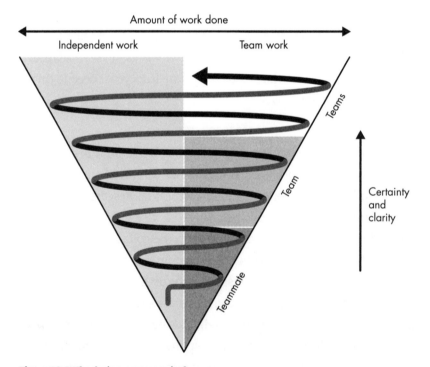

Figure 10-1: The design process spiral

With every iteration, the design document becomes clearer and more detailed. The author's confidence in the solution grows, as does the body of work behind the design—experiments, proofs of concept, and benchmarks. The number and variety of people consulted about the design also grows over time.

You begin at the base of the cone. You are unclear about the problem space, requirements, and possible solutions. So early in the process, it is impossible for you to have a solution that you're confident in.

As you research, you bounce back and forth between independent work and discussion with a small group of teammates or experts in the domain you're researching. You brainstorm and experiment. The goal is to learn—to increase certainty and clarity.

Eventually, your research, experimentation, and brainstorming leads you to a preferred design. After sanity-checking it with those you've been working with, you write a design document. As you write, you discover more unknowns. You create a few small prototypes to validate your designs, answer questions, and help choose between viable alternative approaches. You conduct more research and ask experts for their input. You flesh out a draft of the design document.

The arrow in the cone spirals further upward. You are now more certain that you understand the problem space. Your prototypes provide increasing confidence in your solution. You have a design proposal and are ready to circulate it. You share it with your team and get still more feedback. You research, discuss, and update your design document.

You're at the highest level of the cone now. Significant work has been invested in your design, and you are confident in your approach. You circulate the design across your organization. Security, operations, adjacent teams, and architects all need to be made aware of the changes you're committing to, not just to give feedback but to update their mental model of how the system works.

After your design is approved, implementation begins, but design isn't over. Implementation will surface more surprises. You must update your design document if any large deviations are made as you and your team code.

Thinking About Design

The base of the design funnel begins with exploration. You need to understand the problem space and requirements before you can develop a design. Exploration requires thinking, research, experimentation, and discussion. As the funnel suggests, exploration is both an individual and a team sport.

Define the Problem

Your first task is to define and understand the problem (or problems) that you're trying to solve. You need to understand the boundaries of the problem to know how to solve it and to avoid building the wrong thing. You might even discover there is no problem or that the problem isn't worth solving.

Start by asking stakeholders what they perceive the problem to be. These stakeholders may be your manager, teammates, product managers, or tech leads. Not everyone will perceive the problem the same way.

Restate the problem, in your own words, back to the stakeholders. Ask if your understanding matches theirs. If there is more than one problem, ask which problems are the highest priority.

"What happens if we don't solve this problem?" is a powerful question. When the stakeholder answers, ask if the outcome is acceptable. You'll find many problems don't actually need to be solved.

Once you've collected notes on the problem from various stakeholders, try to synthesize the feedback into a clear problem statement. Don't take problem descriptions at face value. Think critically about what you've been told. Pay particular attention to the scope of the problem—what's included and what could be included but isn't. Don't take the union of all problems from all stakeholders; this will get unwieldy. Don't be afraid to trim low-priority changes. Write and circulate the problem statement—both what's in and out of scope—to validate your understanding and get feedback.

The initial feature request might look like this:

Supply managers want to see catalog and page numbers for each item listed on the inventory page. Showing catalog information will make it easier to reorder items when supplies run low. We can use contract labor to scan all catalogs, and we can use an ML model to map scanned images to item descriptions in the database.

This request will trigger a lot of questions to the product manager:

- How do supply managers place orders now?
- Can an item show up in multiple catalogs?
- How are the users addressing their need without this feature?
- What are the pain points of the current solution?
- Which of these pain points has the biggest impact on the business?

Answers to these questions might lead to a revised problem statement:

Supply room managers need an easy way to reorder items when supplies run low. Currently, they maintain a mapping of the stock entry identifiers we generate to the vendor's name and SKU in Excel spreadsheets and cross-reference them. Going from our software to Excel for lookups to ordering from a vendor is both slow and error prone.

There can be multiple vendors for a single SKU. Supply room managers prefer to have access to all of them so they can minimize cost. They currently track a single vendor per item due to spreadsheet limitations.

The supply room managers rank their priorities in the following order: data accuracy, time to place an order, and order cost minimization.

Several vendors offer online catalogs, and about half offer online purchasing.

The refined problem description will lead to a very different solution than the original. The engineer is focusing on the problem and enumerating priorities. Proposed solutions like the contract work and machine learning model have been discarded. Information about online vendor catalogs has also been included to inform potential solutions.

Do Your Research

Don't go straight from problem definition to "final" design. Consider relevant research, alternative solutions, and trade-offs. The design you come up with should be not your first idea but your best.

There is a plethora of resources online. Look at how others solved similar problems. Many companies run engineering blogs that describe how they solve problems and implement their features. While company blogs are partially a marketing exercise and often describe simplified architectures that elide the tricky bits, blog posts are still a reasonable way to get a general sense for what others are doing. Contacting the authors through social networks or email may supply details that didn't make it into the blog post.

Industry conferences are another resource to check. Slide decks or recordings are usually posted online. And don't forget about academic research and white papers; use the references section at the end of a paper to find yet more reading material.

Talk to experts in the problem space that you're exploring. Ask experts in your company for input, but don't limit yourself to your coworkers. You'll find that many blog and paper authors and presenters are eager to talk about their work. Just be careful not to divulge proprietary company information when talking to outsiders.

Finally, think critically. Not everything you read online is a good idea. A particularly common misstep is to take a solution for a problem that is similar but not identical to yours and to copy it wholesale. Your problems aren't Google's (possibly even if you work for Google) even though they look similar.

Conduct Experiments

Experiment with your ideas by writing draft code and running tests. Write draft APIs and partial implementations. Run performance tests or even A/B user tests to learn how systems and users behave.

Experiments will give you confidence in your ideas, expose design trade-offs, and clarify the problem space. You'll also get a feel for how your code will be used. Circulate your prototypes with your team to get feedback.

Don't get attached to your experimental code. Proof-of-concept code is meant to illustrate an idea and be thrown away or rewritten. Focus your efforts on illustrating or testing your idea. Don't write tests or spend time polishing code. You're trying to learn as much as you can as quickly as possible.

Give It Time

Good design takes creativity. Don't expect to sit down and bang out a design in one shot. Give yourself large chunks of time, take breaks, change your scenery, and be patient.

Design requires deep thought. You can't do design in 15-minute increments; give yourself several hours to focus. Paul Graham wrote an essay entitled "Manager's Schedule, Maker's Schedule" (*http://www.paulgraham .com/makersschedule.html*). The post describes how valuable uninterrupted time is to "makers"—that's you. Figure out when you are most able to sustain deep concentration and block off the time on your calendar. Chris prefers quiet after-lunch design sessions, while Dmitriy feels most productive in the early morning. Find the time that works for you and protect it.

Interruptions are a deep-work killer. Avoid all means of communication: close chat, turn off email, disable phone notifications, and maybe sit in a different spot. Make sure you have the tools you need—whiteboard, notebook, papers—if you switch locations.

You're not going to be "designing" the entire time you've blocked time off. Your brain needs time to relax. Take breaks, and give yourself room to breathe. Allow your mind to relax and wander. Go for a walk, make some tea, read, write, and draw diagrams.

Design is a 24-hour-a-day gig, so be patient. Your brain is always mulling ideas. Thoughts will come to you randomly throughout the day (and even while you sleep).

A relaxed approach to design doesn't mean you can take forever. You have delivery dates to meet. Design spikes are a good way to manage the tension between creative work and predictable delivery. A *spike* is an Extreme Programming (XP) term for a time-bounded investigation. Allocating a spike task in a sprint will give you space to do deep thought without having other tasks to worry about.

Writing Design Documents

Design documents are a scalable way to clearly communicate your ideas. The process of writing structures your thinking and highlights areas of weakness. Documenting your ideas does not always come naturally. To create useful design documents, focus on the most consequential changes, keep the goal and the audience in mind, practice writing, and keep your documents up-to-date.

Document Consequential Changes

Not every change requires a design document, much less a formal design review process. Your organization may have its own guidelines for this; absent those, use these three criteria to decide if a design document is required:

- The project will require at least a month of engineering work.

- The change will have long-lasting implications with regard to extending and maintaining the software.

- The change will significantly impact other teams.

The first case is self-evident: if the project will take a while to implement, it's a good idea to spend some up-front time on writing down the design to ensure you're not heading down the wrong path.

The second case needs a little more explanation. Some changes are quick to introduce but come with long-term ramifications. This might be introducing a new piece of infrastructure—a caching layer, a network proxy, or a storage system. It might be a new public API or security measure. While there may be a fast way to add them to solve some immediate problem, such changes tend to have long-term costs that may not be obvious. Going through the process of writing the design document and getting it reviewed will give concerns a chance to surface and get addressed. A review will also ensure the whole team understands what is being added and why, which will help avoid surprises down the line.

Changes that significantly impact many teams also need a design document. Teams need to know what you're doing so they can provide feedback and so they can accommodate your changes. Changes that have broad reach often require code reviews or refactoring, and other designs might be impacted. Your design document notifies teams of your forthcoming changes.

Know Why You're Writing

Superficially, design documents tell others how a software component works. But a design document's function exceeds simple documentation. A design document is a tool to help you think, to get feedback, to keep your team informed, to ramp up new engineers, and to drive project planning.

Writing has a way of exposing what you don't know (trust us on this one). Pushing yourself to write down your design forces you to explore the problem space and crystallize your ideas. You'll have to confront alternative approaches and gaps in understanding. It's a turbulent process, but you'll have a better understanding of your design and its trade-offs for having gone through it. The clarity of thought you'll get from writing down your design will make design discussions more productive as well.

It's easier to solicit feedback on a written design. Written documents can be widely circulated, and others can read and respond on their own time. Even when feedback is minimal, circulating a design document keeps the team informed.

Spreading design knowledge will help others maintain an accurate mental model of how the system works. The team will make better design and implementation decisions later. On-call engineers will correctly understand how the system is behaving. Engineers can also use design documents to learn from their teammates.

Design documents are particularly helpful for engineers new to the team. Without design documents, engineers find themselves crawling through code, creating box diagrams, and teasing knowledge out of senior engineers to understand what's going on. Reading a trove of design documents is far more efficient.

Finally, managers and tech leads use design documents for project planning. Many design documents include milestones or implementation steps needed to complete the project. Having a concrete design written down makes it easier to coordinate with other teams if a project is cross-functional.

Learn to Write

Engineers who feel they aren't good writers can be intimidated by the prospect of writing; don't be. Writing is a skill, and like any other skill, it is developed through practice. Take advantage of opportunities to write—design documents, emails, code review comments—and try hard to write clearly.

Writing clearly will make your life much easier. Writing is a lossy method of information transfer: you're taking your ideas and writing them down, and your teammates are reconstituting your ideas imperfectly in their minds. Good writing improves the fidelity of this transfer. Good writing is also a career builder. A well-written document is easily circulated to large groups, including executives, and strong writers do not go unnoticed.

Reread what you've written from the perspective of the target audience: it doesn't matter if you understand it; what matters is if they understand it. Be concise. To help get a reader's perspective, read what others have written. Think about how you would edit their writing: what's extra, what's missing. Seek out good document writers in your company and ask for feedback on what you've written. See "Level Up" for more writing resources.

Developers who aren't native language speakers sometimes feel intimidated by written communication. Software engineering is a global trade. It's rare that everyone on a team will be speaking their native tongue. Don't let language barriers discourage you from writing design documents. Don't worry about having perfect grammar; what matters is expressing your thoughts clearly.

Keep Design Documents Up-to-Date

We've been talking about design documents as a tool to propose and finalize a design before it's implemented. Once you begin implementation, design documents morph from proposals into documents that describe how software is implemented: they are *living documents*.

Two common pitfalls occur during the transition from proposal to documentation. The first pitfall is that the proposal document is abandoned and never updated again. Implementations diverge, and the document is misleading to future users. The second pitfall is that the document is updated, and the history of the proposal is lost. Future developers can't see discussions that led to design decisions and might repeat mistakes of the past.

Keep your documents up-to-date as you go. If your design proposals and design documents are two separate things (like Python PEPs versus Python documentation), you'll need to keep the documentation up-to-date with implemented proposals. Make sure others keep documents updated as you conduct code reviews.

Version control your design documents. A good trick is to keep design documents version controlled in the same repository as code. Code reviews can then be used as a review for design comments. The documents can also be updated as code evolves. Not everyone likes to review design documents in Markdown or AsciiDoc, though; if you prefer a wiki, Google Docs, or Word, keep the entire history of the document available, including discussions.

Using a Design Document Template

A design document should describe the current code design, the motivation for a change, potential solutions, and a proposed solution. The document should include details about the proposed solution: architectural diagrams, important algorithmic details, public APIs, schemas, trade-offs with alternatives, assumptions, and dependencies.

There isn't a one-size-fits-all template for design documents, but open source design documents are a way to see how major changes get documented. We've included links to Python Enhancement Proposals, Kafka Improvement Proposals, and Rust Request for Comments (RFCs) in the "Level Up" section at the end of this chapter. Use your team's template if they have one; if not, try this structure, which we'll describe in detail:

- Introduction
- Current State and Context

- Motivation for Change

- Requirements

- Potential Solutions

- Proposed Solution

- Design and Architecture

  - System Diagram

  - UI/UX Changes

  - Code Changes

  - API Changes

  - Persistence Layer Changes

- Test Plan

- Rollout Plan

- Unresolved Questions

- Appendix

Introduction

Introduce the problem being solved and say why it is worth solving. Provide a paragraph-long summary of the proposed change and some guidance that points different readers—security engineers, operations engineers, data scientists—to relevant sections.

Current State and Context

Describe the architecture that is being modified and define terminology. Explain what systems with nonobvious names do: "Feedler is our user sign-up system. It's built on top of Rouft, infrastructure that provides stateful workflow processing." Talk about the ways in which the issue is currently being addressed. Are there workarounds being employed? What are their drawbacks?

Motivation for Change

Software teams tend to have more projects than they can tackle at once. Why is this particular problem worth solving, and why now? Describe the benefits that will result from this effort. Tie these benefits to business needs: "We can reduce the memory footprint by 50 percent" is not as strong as "By reducing the memory needs by 50 percent, we can address the most common objection to installing our software, leading to greater adoption." But be careful not to overpromise!

Requirements

List requirements that an acceptable solution must meet. These can be broken out into sections such as the following:

- **User-facing requirements:** These are usually the bulk of the requirements. They define the nature of the change from a user perspective.

- **Technical requirements:** These include hard requirements on the solution that must be met. Technical requirements are usually caused by interoperability concerns or strict internal guidelines, such as "Must support MySQL for the storage layer" or "Must provide an OpenAPI spec to work with our application gateway." Service level objectives can also be defined here.

- **Security and compliance requirements:** Though these might be seen as user-facing or technical requirements, they are often broken out separately to ensure that security needs are explicitly discussed. Data retention and access policies are often covered here.

- **Other:** This can include critical deadlines, budgets, and other important considerations.

Potential Solutions

There are usually multiple ways one can solve a problem. Writing this section is as much a tool for you as the reader; it's meant to force you to think through not just your first idea but alternative ideas and their trade-offs. Describe reasonable alternative approaches and why you dismissed them. Describing potential solutions will preemptively address "Why not do X?" comments. And if you've dismissed a solution for the wrong reasons, commenters have a chance to catch a misunderstanding. Readers might even identify alternatives you hadn't considered.

Proposed Solution

Describe the solution you settled on. This description goes into more detail than the very brief description in the introduction and may contain diagrams that highlight changes. Here and in the following sections, if your proposal includes multiple phases, explain how the solution evolves from phase to phase.

Design and Architecture

Design and architecture normally make up the bulk of the document. All the technical minutiae worth discussing go here. Highlight implementation details of interest, such as key libraries and frameworks being leveraged, implementation patterns, and any departures from common company practices. Design and architecture should include block diagrams of components, call and data flow, UI, code, API, and schema mock-ups.

SYSTEM DIAGRAM

Include a diagram that shows the main components and how they interact. Explain what is changing by highlighting new and changed components or creating before and after diagrams. The diagram should be accompanied by prose that walks the reader through the changes.

UI/UX CHANGES

Create mock-ups if your project changes user interfaces. Use the mocks to walk through a user's activity flow. If your change does not have a visual component, this section might talk about developer experience with the library you are creating or ways a user might use your command line tool. The goal is to think through the experience of the people who will interact with your change.

Code Changes

Describe your implementation plan. Highlight what, how, and when existing code will need to change. Describe any new abstractions that need to be introduced.

API Changes

Document changes to existing APIs and any newly proposed APIs. Discuss backward/forward compatibility and versioning. Remember to include error handling in your API proposal: it should respond with useful information when encountering malformed inputs, constraint violations, and unexpected internal errors or exceptions.

Persistence Layer Changes

Explain storage technologies being introduced or modified. Discuss new databases, file and filesystem layouts, search indices, and data transformation pipelines. Include all schema changes and notes on their backward compatibility.

Test Plan

Do not define every test in advance; rather, explain how you plan to verify your changes. Discuss sourcing or generating test data, highlight use cases that need to be covered, discuss libraries and testing strategies you expect to leverage, and explain how you will validate that security requirements are met.

Rollout Plan

Describe the strategies you'll use to avoid complicated deployment ordering requirements. Document the feature flags you will need to put in place to control the rollout and whether you will use deployment patterns from Chapter 8. Think about how you would find out if changes are *not* working and how you will roll back if problems are discovered.

Unresolved Questions

Explicitly list pressing questions that have not yet been answered in the design. This is a good way to solicit input from your readers and to state your "known unknowns."

Appendix

Put extra details of interest in the appendix. This is also a good place to add references to related work and further reading.

Collaborating on Design

Constructively collaborating with your team will lead to a better design. But collaboration isn't always easy. Developers are an opinionated bunch. Interpreting and condensing feedback into a meaningful design isn't easy. Collaborate on design by working within your team's design processes, communicating early and often to avoid surprises, and using design discussions to brainstorm.

Understand Your Team's Design Review Process

Design reviews notify architects of large upcoming changes and give leads a chance to provide feedback. Some organizations have robust review policies, while others are more informal. Architectural review boards and "request for decision" processes are two of the more common patterns.

Architectural reviews are more formal, heavier-weight processes. Designs must be approved by outside stakeholders such as operations and security members. A design document is required, and there might be multiple rounds of meetings or presentations. Because of their high time cost, architectural reviews are reserved for large or risky changes.

Don't wait on final approval before writing code. Spend time implementing prototypes and proof-of-concept "spikes" to increase confidence in the design and to give you a shorter path to production. But don't go beyond proof-of-concept work. You'll probably have to change your code based on design feedback.

We call the other type of design review process *request for decision*, or *RFD* (not to be confused with the Internet Society request for comment process, the RFC). The term RFD is not very common, but the pattern is; RFDs are fast intrateam reviews to quickly reach decisions that need some discussion but not a full review. An engineer requesting a decision circulates a quick write-up describing the decision to be made—a lightweight design document. Teammates then whiteboard, discuss their options, provide input, and make a decision.

There are, of course, other design review patterns. What's important is that you understand which processes your team follows. Missing a design review step can cause your project to get derailed at the last moment. Find out who has to be informed or sign off on your design work and who is empowered to make decisions.

Don't Surprise People

Gently and incrementally ease people into your design proposal. You're setting yourself up for failure if a formal design document is the first time other teams and tech leads learn of your work. Each party has a different point of view and a different set of interests and may react strongly to a sudden design document that they had no say in.

Instead, when you do your initial research, get early feedback from other teams and tech leads; this will lead to a better design, keep them aware of your work, and give them a stake in your design. The parties you involve early can become champions of your work later.

Feedback sessions don't need to be formal or scheduled. Casual conversations over lunch, in a hallway, or before meetings start are fine— even preferred. Your goal is simply to make people aware of what you're

---

doing, to give an opportunity for feedback, and to get them thinking about your work.

Keep people up-to-date as you progress. Give updates in status meetings and standups. Continue having casual conversations. Pay attention to second-order effects your proposed changes might have and whom this might impact; notify affected teams of upcoming changes. This goes for support, QA, and operational teams in particular. Be inclusive—pull people into brainstorming sessions and listen to their thoughts.

Brainstorm with Design Discussions

Design discussions help you understand a problem space, share knowledge, discuss trade-offs, and solidify design. These brainstorming sessions are informal, conversation is free flowing, and whiteboards are filled with ink. Discussions happen early in the design cycle, when the problem is reasonably well understood but the design is not yet settled; a draft design document should exist, but it may still have a lot of gaps and open questions. Break brainstorming into multiple sessions with different participants, focusing on different aspects of the design.

Brainstorming sessions range in size from two to about five. Opt for larger, more inclusive brainstorming sessions when a problem is particularly multifaceted or controversial. For more straightforward discussions, keep the number of invitees small to make the conversation flow easier.

Design discussion meetings need to be scheduled for large chunks of time—two hours or so. Ideas need time to develop. Try not to cut discussions short; let people run out of ideas or simply get exhausted. You might need more than one brainstorming session to reach a conclusion.

Before the brainstorming session, develop a loose agenda that includes the problem, scope, and proposed design (or designs), along with potential trade-offs and open questions. Participants are expected to read the agenda beforehand, so keep it brief. The purpose is to provide enough information to get a free-flowing discussion started.

In the session itself, don't impose too much structure; people need to jump around to explore ideas. Use a whiteboard rather than a slide deck, and speak extemporaneously if possible. (It's okay to refer to notes, though.)

Note-taking can be a distraction during brainstorming sessions. Some teams formally designate a notetaker for a meeting. Make sure that this role is evenly shared by all team members or the perpetual note-taker won't be able to contribute. The whiteboard is also a note keeper; take pictures as the discussion progresses, or save intermediate states if using a virtual board. After the meeting, write a summary based on your recollection, using the whiteboard images as your guide. Send the notes to the attendees and other relevant teammates.

Contribute to Design

You should contribute to your team's design work, not just your own. As with code reviews, contributing to design can feel uncomfortable. You might think you have nothing to contribute to designs from more senior developers. Reading design documents and going to brainstorming meetings might feel like a distraction. Do it anyway. Your participation will improve your team's design and help you learn.

When you join in on design, give suggestions and ask questions. Apply the same guidance we give for code reviews. Think holistically about the design. Consider security, maintainability, performance, scale, and so on. Pay special attention to how designs impact your areas of expertise. Communicate clearly and be respectful.

Asking questions is as important as giving suggestions. Questions will help you to grow. As in the classroom, you're probably not the only person wondering about a design decision, so your questions help others grow, too. Moreover, your questions might trigger new ideas or expose gaps in the design that hadn't been considered.

Do's and Don'ts

DO'S	DON'TS
DO use a design document template.	**DON'T** get attached to experimental code; it will change.
DO read blogs, papers, and presentations to get ideas.	**DON'T** explore only one solution.
DO think critically about everything that you read.	**DON'T** let a non-native language deter you from writing.
DO experiment with code during design.	**DON'T** forget to update design documents if the implementation diverges from the plan.
DO learn to write clearly, and practice often.	**DON'T** be reluctant to participate in team design discussions.
DO version control design documents.	
DO ask questions about teammate's designs.	

Level Up

Richard Hickey, author of Clojure, gives a "field report" on software design in his talk "Hammock Driven Development" (*https://youtu.be/f84n5oFoZBc/*). Hickey's talk is one of the best introductions we've seen to the messy process of software design.

Use large open source projects to see real-world design in progress. Python Enhancement Proposals (*https://github.com/python/peps/*), Kafka Improvement Proposals (*https://cwiki.apache.org/confluence/display/KAFKA/Kafka+Improvement+Proposals/*), and Rust Request for Comments (RFCs) (*https://github.com/rust-lang/rfcs/*) are good illustrations of real-world design.

For a glimpse of internal design processes, WePay's engineering blog has a post, "Effective Software Design Documents" (*https://wecode .wepay.com/posts/effective-software-design-documents*). The post describes WePay's approach to design and how it's evolved over the years. The design template that WePay has used for hundreds of internal designs is available on GitHub (*https://github.com/wepay/design_doc_template/*).

Elements of Style by William Strunk and E.B. White (Auroch Press, 2020) is the canonical reference for clear writing. We also strongly recommend reading *On Writing Well* by William Zissner (Harper Perennial, 2016). Both of these books will dramatically improve your writing clarity. Paul Graham, of Y Combinator fame, has two essays on writing: "How to Write Usefully" (*http://paulgraham.com/useful.html*) and "Write Like You Talk" (*http://www.paulgraham.com/talk.html*).

CREATING EVOLVABLE
ARCHITECTURES

Requirements volatility—changing customer demands—is an unavoidable challenge for software projects. Product requirements and context will change over time; your application must change as well. But changing requirements can cause instability and derail development.

Managers try to deal with requirements volatility using iterative development processes like Agile development (discussed in the next chapter). You can do your part to accommodate changing requirements by building *evolvable architectures*. Evolvable architectures eschew complexity, the enemy of evolvability.

This chapter will teach you techniques that can make your software simpler and thus easier to evolve. Paradoxically, achieving simplicity in software can be difficult; without conscious effort, code will grow tangled and complex. We'll begin by describing complexity and how it leads to rigid and confusing codebases. We'll then show you design principles that reduce complexity. Finally, we'll translate these design principles into concrete API and data layer best practices.

Understanding Complexity

In *A Philosophy of Software Design* (Yaknyam Press, 2018), Stanford computer science professor John Ousterhout writes, "Complexity is anything related to the structure of a system that makes it hard to understand and modify the system." Per Ousterhout, complex systems have two characteristics: high *dependency* and high *obscurity*. We add a third: high *inertia*.

High *dependency* leads software to rely on other code's API or behavior. Dependency is obviously unavoidable and even desirable, but a balance must be struck. Every new connection and assumption makes code harder to change. High-dependency systems are hard to modify because they have *tight coupling* and high *change amplification*. Tight coupling describes modules that depend heavily on one another. It leads to high change amplification, where a single change requires modifications in dependencies as well. Thoughtful API design and a restrained use of abstraction will minimize tight coupling and change amplification.

High *obscurity* makes it difficult for programmers to predict a change's side effects, how code behaves, and where changes need to be made. Obscure code takes longer to learn, and developers are more likely to inadvertently break things. *God objects* that "know" too much, global state that encourages side effects, excessive indirection that obscures code, and *action at distance* that affects behavior in distant parts of the program are all symptoms of high obscurity. APIs with clear contracts and standard patterns reduce obscurity.

Inertia, the characteristic that we've added to Ousterhout's list, is software's tendency to stay in use. Easily discarded code used for a quick experiment has low inertia. A service that powers a dozen business-critical applications has high inertia. Complexity's cost accrues over time, so high-inertia, high-change systems should be simplified, while low-inertia or low-change systems can be left complex (as long as you discard them or continue to leave them alone).

Complexity cannot always be eliminated, but you can choose where to put it. Backward-compatible changes (discussed later) might make code simpler to use but more complicated to implement. Layers of indirection to decouple subsystems reduce dependency but increase obscurity. Be thoughtful about when, where, and how to manage complexity.

Design for Evolvability

Faced with unknown future requirements, engineers usually choose one of two tactics: they try to guess what they'll need in the future, or they build abstractions as an escape hatch to make subsequent code changes easier. Don't play this game; both approaches lead to complexity. Keep things simple (known as KISS—*keep it simple, stupid*—thanks to the US Navy's penchant for acronyms and tough love). Use the KISS mnemonic to remember to build with simplicity in mind. Simple code lets you add complexity later, when the need becomes clear and the change becomes unavoidable.

The easiest way to keep code simple is to avoid writing it altogether. Tell yourself that *you ain't gonna need it (YAGNI)*. When you do write code, use the principle of least astonishment and encapsulation. These design principles will keep your code easy to evolve.

You Ain't Gonna Need It

YAGNI is a deceptively simple design practice: don't build things you don't need. YAGNI violations happen when developers get excited, fixated, or worried about some aspect of their code. It's difficult to predict what you'll need and what you won't. Every wrong guess is wasted effort. After the initial waste, the code continues to bog things down, it needs to be maintained, developers need to understand it, and it must be built and tested.

Luckily, there are a few habits you can build to avoid unnecessary development. Avoid premature optimization, unnecessarily flexible abstractions, and product features that aren't needed for a *minimum viable product (MVP)*—the bare-minimum feature set that you need to get user feedback.

Premature optimization occurs when a developer adds a performance optimization to code before it's proven to be needed. In the classic scenario, a developer sees an area of code that could be made faster or more scalable by adding complex logic and architectural layers such as caches, sharded databases, or queues. The developer optimizes the code before it's been shipped, before anyone has used it. After shipping the code, the developer discovers that the optimization was not needed. Removing optimization never happens, and complexity accrues. Most performance and scalability improvements come with a high complexity cost. For example, a cache is fast, but it can also become inconsistent with underlying data.

Flexible abstractions—plugin architectures, wrapper interfaces, and generic data structures like key-value pairs—are another temptation. Developers think they can easily adjust if some new requirement pops up. But abstraction comes with a cost; it boxes implementations into rigid boundaries that the developer ends up fighting later. Flexibility also makes code harder to read and understand. Take this distributed queuing interface:

```
interface IDistributedQueue {
  void send(String queue, Object message);
  Object receive(String queue);
}
```

IDistributedQueue looks simple enough: you send and receive messages. But what if the underlying queue supports both keys and values for a message (as Apache Kafka does) or message ACKing (as Amazon's Simple Queue Service does)? Developers are faced with a choice: Should the interface be the union of all features from all message queues or the intersection of all features? The union of all features produces an interface where no single implementation works for all methods. The intersection of all features leads to a limited interface that doesn't have enough features to be useful. You're better off directly using an implementation. You can refactor later if you decide you need to support another implementation.

The best way to keep your code flexible is to simply have less of it. For everything you build, ask yourself what is absolutely necessary, and throw away the rest. This technique—called *Muntzing*—will keep your software trim and adaptable.

Adding cool new product features is also tempting. Developers talk themselves into the cool-feature pitfall for a variety of reasons: they mistake their usage for what most users want, they think it'll be easy to add, or they think it'll be neat! Each new feature takes time to build and maintain, and you don't know if the feature will actually be useful.

Building an MVP will keep you honest about what you really need. MVPs allow you to test an idea without investing in a full-fledged implementation.

There are, of course, caveats to YAGNI. As your experience grows, you'll get better at predicting when flexibility and optimization are necessary. In the meantime, place interface shims where you suspect optimizations can be inserted, but don't actually implement them. For example, if you are creating a new file format and suspect you'll need compression or encryption later, provide a header that specifies the encoding, but only implement the uncompressed encoding. You can add compression in the future, and the header will make it easy for new code to read older files.

Principle of Least Astonishment

The *principle of least astonishment* is pretty clear: don't surprise users. Build features that behave as users first expect. Features with a high learning curve or strange behavior frustrate users. Similarly, don't surprise developers. Surprising code is obscure, which causes complexity. You can eliminate surprises by keeping code specific, avoiding implicit knowledge, and using standard libraries and patterns.

Anything nonobvious that a developer needs to know to use an API and is not part of the API itself is considered *implicit knowledge*. APIs that require implicit knowledge will surprise developers, causing bugs and a high learning curve. Two common implicit knowledge violations are hidden ordering requirements and hidden argument requirements.

Ordering requirements dictate that actions take place in a specific sequence. Method ordering is a frequent violation: method A must be called before method B, but the API allows method B to be called first, surprising the developer with a runtime error. Documenting an ordering requirement is good, but it's better not to have one in the first place. Avoid method ordering by having methods invoke submethods:

```
pontoonWorples() {
  if(!flubberized) {
    flubberize()
  }
  // ...
}
```

There are other approaches to avoiding ordering: combining the methods into one, using the *builder pattern*, using the type system and having pontoonWorples work only on FlubberizedWorples rather than all Worples, and so on. All of these are better than requiring your user to know about hidden requirements. If nothing else, you can at least make the method name give developers a heads-up by calling it pontoonFlubberizedWorples(). Counterintuitively, short method and variable names actually increase cognitive load. Specific, longer method names are more descriptive and easier to understand.

Hidden argument requirements occur when a method signature implies a wider range of valid inputs than the method actually accepts. For example, accepting an int while only allowing numbers 1 to 10 is a hidden constraint. Requiring that a certain value field is set in a plain JSON object is also requiring implicit knowledge on the part of the user. Make argument requirements specific and visible. Use specific types that accurately capture your constraints; when using flexible types like JSON, consider using JSON Schema to describe the expected object. At the least, advertise argument requirements in documentation when they can't be made programmatically visible.

Finally, use standard libraries and development patterns. Implementing your own square root method is surprising; using a language's built-in `sqrt()` method is not. The same rule applies for development patterns: use idiomatic code style and development patterns.

Encapsulate Domain Knowledge

Software changes as business requirements change. Encapsulate domain knowledge by grouping software based on business domain—accounting, billing, shipping, and so on. Mapping software components to business domains will keep code changes focused and clean.

Encapsulated domains naturally gravitate toward *high cohesion* and *low coupling*—desirable traits. Highly cohesive software with low coupling is more evolvable because changes tend to have a smaller "blast radius." Code is highly *cohesive* when methods, variables, and classes that relate to one another are near each other in modules or packages. *Decoupled* code is self-contained; a change to its logic does not require changes to other software components.

Developers often think about software in terms of layers: frontend, middle tier, and backend. Layered code is grouped according to technical domain, with all the UI code in one place and all object persistence in another. Grouping code by technical domain works great within a single business domain but grows messy as businesses grow. Separate teams form around each tier, increasing coordination cost since every business logic change slices through all tiers. And shared horizontal layers make it too easy for developers to mix business logic between domains, leading to complex code.

Identifying domain boundaries and encapsulating domain knowledge is as much art as science. There is an entire architectural approach called *Domain-Driven Design (DDD)*, which defines an extensive set of concepts and practices to map business concepts to software. Full-blown DDD is necessary only for the most complex situations. Still, familiarizing yourself with DDD will help you make better design decisions.

Evolvable APIs

As requirements change, you'll need to change your APIs, the shared interfaces between code. Changing an API is easy to do, but it's hard to do right. Many small, rational changes can lead to a sprawling mess. Worse, a minor API change can completely break compatibility. If an API changes in an incompatible way, clients will break; these breakages may not be immediately obvious, especially changes that break at runtime, not during compilation. APIs that are small, clearly defined, compatible, and versioned will be easier to use and evolve.

Keep APIs Small

Small APIs are easier to understand and evolve. Larger APIs put more cognitive load on developers, and you'll have more code to document, support, debug, and maintain. Every new method or field grows the API and locks you further into a specific usage pattern.

Apply the YAGNI philosophy: only add API methods or fields that are immediately needed. When creating an API data model, only add methods you need at the time. When bootstrapping your API using a framework or generator tool, eliminate fields or methods you're not using.

API methods with a lot of fields should have sensible defaults. Developers can focus on relevant fields knowing they'll inherit defaults for the others. Defaults make large APIs feel small.

Expose Well-Defined Service APIs

Evolvable systems have clearly defined request and response schemas that are versioned and have clear compatibility contracts. Schema definitions should be published so they can be used to automatically test both client and server code (see "Package Different Resources Separately" in Chapter 8 for more).

Use standard tools to define service APIs. A well-defined service will declare its schemas, request and response methods, and exceptions. OpenAPI is commonly used for RESTful services, while non-REST services use Protocol Buffers, Thrift, or a similar *interface definition language (IDL)*. Well-defined service APIs make compile-time validation easier and keep clients, servers, and documentation in sync.

Interface definition tools come with code generators that convert service definitions to client and server code. Documentation can also be generated, and test tools can use IDLs to generate stubs and mock data. Some tools even have discoverability features to find services, learn who maintains them, and show how the service is used.

Use your company's API definition framework if they've already chosen one; choosing a "better" one will require too much interoperability work. If your company still hand-rolls REST APIs and the JSON interfaces are evolved in code without a formal spec, your best bet is OpenAPI, as it can be retrofitted on preexisting REST services and does not require major migrations to adopt.

Keep API Changes Compatible

Keeping API changes compatible lets client and server versions evolve independently. There are two forms of compatibility to consider: forward and backward.

Forward-compatible changes allow clients to use a new version of an API when invoking an older service version. A web service that's running version 1.0 of an API but can receive calls from a client using version 1.1 of the API is forward compatible.

Backward-compatible changes are the opposite: new versions of the library or service do not require changes in older client code. A change is backward compatible if code developed against version 1.0 of an API continues to compile and run when used with version 1.1.

Let's take a look at a simple gRPC Hello World service API defined with Protocol Buffers:

```
service Greeter {
  rpc SayHello (HelloRequest) returns (HelloReply) {}
}

message HelloRequest {
  string name = 1;
  int32 favorite_number = 2;
}

message HelloReply {
  string message = 1;
}
```

The Greeter service has one method, called SayHello, which receives a HelloRequest and returns a HelloReply with a fun message about favorite_number. The numbers next to each field are *field ordinals*; Protocol Buffers internally refer to fields using numbers rather than strings.

Suppose we decide to send our greeting over email. We'd need to add an email field:

```
message HelloRequest {
  string name = 1;
  int32 favorite_number = 2;
  required string email = 3;
}
```

This is a *backward-incompatible* change because old clients don't supply an email. When a client invokes the new SayHello with the old HelloRequest, the email will be missing, so the service can't parse the request. Removing the `required` keyword and skipping emails when no address is supplied will maintain backward compatibility.

Required fields are such an evolvability problem that they were removed from Protocol Buffers v3. Kenton Varda, the primary author of Protocol Buffers v2, said, "The 'required' keyword in Protocol Buffers turned out to be a horrible mistake" (*https://capnproto.org/faq.html#how-do-i-make -a-field-required-like-in-protocol-buffers*). Many other systems have required fields, so be careful, and remember, "Required is forever."

We can create a *forward-incompatible* change by tweaking `Hello Request`. Perhaps we want to accommodate negative favorite numbers. The Protocol Buffer documentation reads, "If your field is likely to have negative values, use `sint32` instead," so we change the type of `favorite _number` accordingly:

```
message HelloRequest {
  string name = 1;
  sint32 favorite_number = 2;
}
```

Changing `int32` to `sint32` is both backward and forward incompatible. A client with the new `HelloRequest` will encode `favorite_number` using a different serialization scheme than an old version of `Greeter`, so the service will fail to parse it; and the new version of `Greeter` will fail to parse messages from old clients!

The `sint32` change can be made forward compatible by adding a new field. Protocol Buffers let us rename fields as long as the field number remains the same.

```
message HelloRequest {
  string name = 1;
  int32 _deprecated_favorite_number = 2;
  sint32 favorite_number = 3;
}
```

The server code needs to handle both fields for as long as the old clients are supported. Once rolled out, we can monitor how often clients use the deprecated field and clean up once clients upgrade or a deprecation schedule expires.

Our example uses Protocol Buffers because they have a strongly typed system, and type compatibility is more straightforward to demonstrate and reason about. The same problems occur in other contexts, including "simple" REST services. When client and server content expectations diverge, errors crop up no matter what format you're using. Moreover, it's not just the message fields you need to worry about: a change in *semantics* of the message, or the logic of what happens when certain events transpire, can also be backward or forward incompatible.

Version APIs

As APIs evolve over time, you will need to decide how to handle compatibility across multiple versions. Fully backward- and forward-compatible changes interoperate with all previous and future versions of an API; this can be hard to maintain, creating *cruft* like the logic for dealing with deprecated fields. Less stringent compatibility guarantees allow for more radical changes.

Eventually, you'll want to change your API in a way that isn't compatible with old clients—requiring a new field, for example. Versioning your APIs means you introduce a new version when changes are made. Old clients can continue using the old API version. Tracking versions also helps you communicate with your customers—they can tell you what version they're using, and you can market new features with a new version.

API versions are usually managed with an API gateway or a service mesh. Versioned requests are routed to the appropriate service: a v2 request will be routed to a v2.X.X service instance, while a v3 request will be routed to a v3.X.X service instance. Absent a gateway, clients invoke RPC calls directly to version-specific service hosts, or a single service instance runs multiple versions internally.

API versioning comes with a cost. Older major versions of the service need to be maintained, and bug fixes need to be backported to prior versions. Developers need to keep track of which versions support which features. Lack of version management tooling can push version management on to engineers.

Be pragmatic about versioning methodologies. Semantic versioning, discussed in Chapter 5, is a common API versioning scheme, but many companies version APIs using dates or other numeric schemes. Version numbers can be specified in URI paths, query parameters, or HTTP Accept headers, or using a myriad of other techniques. There are trade-offs between all of these approaches, and a lot of strong opinions. Defer to whatever the standard is at your company; if there isn't one, ask your manager and tech leads for their thoughts on what's best.

Keep documentation versioned along with your APIs. Developers dealing with older versions of your code need accurate documentation. It's really confusing for users to reference a different version of the documentation and discover that the API they're using doesn't match up. Committing API documentation in the main code repository helps to keep documentation and code in sync. Pull requests for code can update documentation as they change APIs and behavior.

API versioning is most valuable when client code is hard to change. You'll usually have the least control over external (customer) clients, so customer-facing APIs are the most important to version. If your team controls both the service and client, you might be able to get away without internal API versioning.

Evolvable Data

APIs are more ephemeral than persisted data; once the client and server APIs are upgraded, the work is done. Data must be evolved as applications change. Data evolution runs the gamut from simple schema changes such as adding or removing a column to rewriting records with new schemas, fixing corruption, rewriting to match new business logic, and massive migrations from one database to another.

Isolating databases and using explicit schemas will make data evolution more manageable. With an isolated database, you need only worry about the impact of a change on your own application. Schemas protect you from reading or writing malformed data, and automated schema migrations make schema changes predictable.

Isolate Databases

Shared databases are difficult to evolve and will result in a loss of *autonomy*—a developer's or team's ability to make independent changes to the system. You will not be able to safely modify schemas, or even read and write, without worrying about how everyone is using your database. The architecture grows brittle as schemas become an unofficial, deeply entrenched API. Separate application databases make changes easier.

Isolated databases are accessed by only a single application, while shared databases are accessed by more than one (see Figure 11-1).

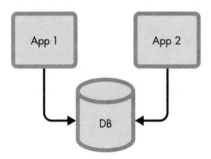

Figure 11-1: Shared databases

Shared databases present several problems. Applications with shared databases can grow to depend directly on each other's data. Applications act as a control point for the underlying data they serve. You can't apply business logic on your raw data before serving it, and you can't easily redirect queries to a new data store during a migration if queries bypass your application. If there are multiple applications writing, the meaning (*semantics*) of the data might diverge, making it harder for readers to reason about. Application data is not protected, so other applications might mutate it in unexpected ways. Schemas aren't isolated; a change in one application's schema can impact others. Nor is performance isolated, so if an application overwhelms the database, all other applications will be affected. In some cases, security boundaries might be violated.

By contrast, isolated databases have just a single reader and writer (see Figure 11-2). All other traffic goes through remote procedural calls.

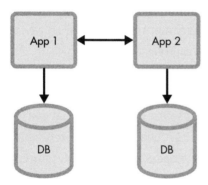

Figure 11-2: *Isolated databases*

Isolated databases afford you all of the flexibility and isolation that shared databases do not. You need only worry about your own application when making database schema changes, and database performance is governed by your usage.

There are occasional cases where a shared database is valuable. When breaking a monolith up, sharing a database serves as a useful intermediate step before data has been migrated to a new isolated database. Managing many databases comes at a high operational cost. Early on, it might make sense to co-locate many databases on the same machines. But make sure any shared databases eventually get isolated and split up or replaced.

Use Schemas

Rigid predefined columns and types, and the heavyweight processes for evolving them, have led to the emergence of popular *schemaless* data management. Most modern datastores support storing JSON or JSON-like objects without predeclaring its structure. Schemaless doesn't literally mean "no schema" (data would be unusable); rather, schemaless data has an implicit schema that is supplied or inferred at read time.

In practice, we've found that a schemaless approach has significant data integrity and complexity problems. A strongly typed schema-forward approach decreases the obscurity, and therefore complexity, of your application. The short-term simplicity is not usually worth the obscurity trade-off. Like code itself, data is sometimes described as "write once, read many"; use schemas to make reads easier.

You'd think not having a schema would make a change easier: you simply start or stop writing fields as you need to evolve data. Schemaless data actually makes changes harder because you don't know what you're breaking as you evolve your data. Data quickly becomes an unintelligible hodgepodge of different record types. Developers, business analysts, and data scientists struggle to keep up. It's going to be a tough day for the data scientist that wants to parse this JSON data:

```
{"name": "Fred", "location": [37.33, -122.03], "enabled": true}
{"name": "Li", "enabled": "false"}
{"name": "Willa", "location": "Boston, MA", "enabled": 0}
```

Defining explicit schemas for your data will keep your application stable and make your data usable. Explicit schemas let you sanity-check data as it is written. Parsing data using explicit schemas is usually faster, too. Schemas also help you detect when forward- and backward-incompatible changes are made. Data scientists know what to expect with data in the following table.

```
CREATE TABLE users (
  id BIGINT AUTO_INCREMENT PRIMARY KEY,
  name VARCHAR(100) NOT NULL,
  latitude DECIMAL,
  longitude DECIMAL,
  enabled BOOLEAN NOT NULL
);
```

The rigidity of explicit schemas also carries a cost: they can be difficult to change. This is by design. Schemas force you to slow down and think through how existing data is going to be migrated and how downstream users will be affected.

Don't hide schemaless data inside schematized data. It's tempting to be lazy and stuff a JSON string into a field called "data" or define a map of strings to contain arbitrary key-value pairs. Hiding schemaless data is self-defeating; you get all of the pain of explicit schemas but none of the gain.

There are some cases where a schemaless approach is warranted. If your primary goal is to move fast—perhaps before you know what you need, when you are iterating rapidly, or when old data has little to no value—a schemaless approach lets you cut corners. Some data is legitimately nonuniform; some records have certain fields that others don't. Flipping data from explicit to implicit schema is also a helpful trick when migrating data; you might temporarily make data schemaless to ease the transition to a new explicit schema.

Automate Schema Migrations

Changing a database's schema is dangerous. A minor tweak—adding an index or dropping a column—can cause the entire database or application to grind to a halt. Managing database changes by manually executing *database description language (DDL)* commands directly on the database is error prone. Database schemas in different environments diverge, the state of the database is uncertain, no one knows who changed what when, and performance impacts are unclear. The mix of error-prone changes and the potential for major downtime is an explosive combination.

Database schema management tools make database changes less error prone. Automated tooling does two things for you: it forces you to track the entire history of a schema, and it gives you tools to migrate a schema from one version to another. Track schema changes, use automated database tools, and work with your database team to manage schema evolution.

The entire history of a schema is usually kept in a series of files defining every change from the initial creation of a schema all the way to its current form. Tracking DDL changes in files helps developers see how the schema has changed over time. Files tracked in a version control system will show who made which changes, when, and why. Pull requests will afford the opportunity for schema reviews and linting.

We can take our users table from the "Use Schemas" section and put it in a versioned file for a schema migration tool like Liquibase:

```
--liquibase formatted sql
--changeset criccomini:create-users-table
CREATE TABLE users (
  id BIGINT AUTO_INCREMENT PRIMARY KEY,
  name VARCHAR(100) NOT NULL,
  latitude DECIMAL,
  longitude DECIMAL,
  enabled BOOLEAN NOT NULL
);
--rollback DROP TABLE users
```

We can then define an ALTER in a separate block:

```
--changeset dryaboy:add-email
ALTER TABLE users ADD email VARCHAR(255);
--rollback DROP COLUMN email
```

Liquibase can use these files to upgrade or downgrade schemas through the CLI:

```
$ liquibase update
```

If Liquibase is pointed at an empty database, it will run both the CREATE and ALTER commands. If it's pointed at a database where the CREATE has already been executed, it will run only the ALTER. Tools like Liquibase often track the current version of a database schema in special metadata tables in the database itself, so don't be surprised if you find tables with names like DATABASECHANGELOG or DATABASECHANGELOGLOCK.

In the previous example, the Liquibase command is run from the command line, usually by a *database administrator (DBA)*. Some teams will automate the execution itself through a commit hook or a web UI.

Don't couple database and application lifecycles. Tying schema migrations to application deployment is dangerous. Schema changes are delicate and can have serious performance implications. Separating database migrations from application deployment lets you control when schema changes go out.

Liquibase is just one tool that can manage database migrations; there are others like Flyway and Alembic. Many *object-resource mappers (ORMs)* come with schema migration managers as well. If your company already has one in place, use it; if not, work with the team to figure out what to use. Once selected, use the database migration system for all the changes; circumventing it will negate the tool's benefit since reality has diverged from what's tracked.

More sophisticated database operations tools also exist. Tools like GitHub's gh-ost and Percona's pt-online-schema-change help database administrators run large schema changes without impacting performance. Other tools like Skeema and Square's Shift provide more sophisticated versioning that lets you "diff" database schemas and automatically derive changes. All of these tools help make database evolution safer.

Most migration tools support rollbacks, which undo a migration's changes. Rollbacks can only do so much, so be careful. For example, rolling back a column deletion will recreate a column, but it will not recreate the data that used to be stored in that column! Backing up a table prior to deletion is prudent.

Because of the permanent and large-scale nature of these types of changes, organizations will often have specific subteams responsible for ensuring the changes are done correctly. These might be DBAs, operations or SREs, or a set of senior engineers familiar with the tools, performance implications, and application-specific concerns. These teams are a great resource for understanding the nuances of data storage systems; learn from them.

Maintain Schema Compatibility

Data written to disk has the same compatibility problems that APIs have. Like APIs, the reader and writer of the data can change independently; they might not be the same software and might not be on the same machine. And like APIs, data has a schema with field names and types. Changing schemas in a forward- or backward-incompatible way can break applications. Use schema compatibility checks to detect incompatible changes, and use data products to decouple internal and external schemas.

Developers think databases are an implementation detail that's hidden from other systems. Fully encapsulated databases are ideal but not often realized in practice. Even if a production database is hidden behind an application, the data is often exported to data warehouses.

Data warehouses are databases used for analytic and reporting purposes. Organizations set up an *extract, transform, load (ETL)* data pipeline that extracts data from production databases and transforms and loads it into a data warehouse (see Figure 11-3).

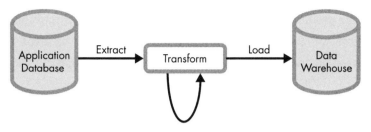

Figure 11-3: *ETL data pipeline*

ETL pipelines depend heavily on database schemas. Simply dropping the column in a production database could cause the entire data pipeline to grind to a halt. Even if dropping a column doesn't break the data pipeline, downstream users might be using the field for reporting, machine learning models, or ad hoc queries.

Other systems might also depend on your database schemas. *Change data capture (CDC)* is an event-based architecture that converts insert, update, and delete operations into messages for downstream consumers. An insert into a "members" table might trigger a message that an email service uses to send an email to the new user. Such messages are an implicit API, and making backward-incompatible schema changes can break other services.

Data warehouse pipelines and downstream users must be protected from breaking schema changes. Validate that your schema changes are safe before executing them in production. Compatibility checks should be done as early as possible, ideally at code commit time by inspecting database DDL statements. Executing DDL statements in a preproduction integration testing environment, if one exists, can also protect changes. Run your DDL statements and integration tests to verify that downstream systems don't break.

You can also protect internal schemas by exporting a *data product* that explicitly decouples internal schemas from downstream users. Data products map internal schemas to separate user-facing schemas; the development team owns both the production database and the published data products. Separate data products, which might simply be database views, allow teams to maintain compatibility with data consumers without having to freeze their internal database schemas.

Do's and Don'ts

DO'S	DON'TS
DO remember YAGNI: "You Ain't Gonna Need It."	**DON'T** build too many abstractions without purpose.
DO use standard libraries and development patterns.	**DON'T** write methods with hidden ordering or argument requirements.
DO use an IDL to define your APIs.	**DON'T** surprise other developers with exotic code.
DO version external APIs and documentation.	**DON'T** make incompatible API changes.
DO isolate application databases from each other.	**DON'T** be dogmatic about internal API versioning.
DO define explicit schemas for all your data.	**DON'T** embed schemaless data in string or byte fields.
DO use migration tools to automate database schema management.	
DO maintain schema compatibility if downstream consumers use your data.	

Level Up

A book-length treatment on evolvable architectures can be found in *Building Evolutionary Architectures*, written by Neal Ford, Rebecca Parsons, and Patrick Kua (O'Reilly Media, 2017). For more depth on evolvable APIs and data, see their work. They discuss DDD briefly; for the full experience, refer to *Implementing Domain Driven Design* by Vaughn Vernon (Addison-Wesley Professional, 2013).

We cite John Ousterhout's work on complexity in the beginning of the chapter. See his excellent (and short) book, *A Philosophy of Software Design* (Yaknyam Press, 2018), to learn more about complexity and how to manage it.

Zach Tellman's *Elements of Clojure* (*lulu.com*, 2019) is a wonderful book that has only four chapters: "Names," "Idioms," "Indirection," and "Composition." It is a lucid, concise discussion of these four topics, which will help you build evolvable architectures (even if you never touch a line of Clojure).

Richard Hickey has a beautiful talk called *Simple Made Easy* (*https://www.youtube.com/watch?v=oytL881p-nQ*). Hickey's talk discusses simplicity, complexity, "easiness," and how to build good software. The talk is a must-watch.

Data Mesh: Building a Next Generation Data Architecture by Zhamak Dehghani (coming out end of 2021) contains a deeper discussion of data products.

Designing Data-Intensive Applications by Martin Kleppman (O'Reilly Media, 2017) is an excellent book that covers, among other things, the subjects of data evolution, data schemas, IDLs, and change data capture. This book is an instant classic, and we highly recommend it.

AGILE PLANNING

Software development should be planned and tracked. Your teammates want to know what you're working on so they can collaborate with you effectively. Teams need to track progress so they can plan future work and course-correct as new information is discovered during development. Without a deliberate process, projects drag on, outside demands steal focus, and operational issues distract developers.

Agile development, a software development methodology, is widely adopted to deliver quality software quickly. Understanding the core philosophy and the goals of common Agile processes such as sprint planning, daily stand-ups, reviews, and retrospectives will help you use them effectively. This chapter introduces you to Agile planning basics and key practices of Scrum (a commonly adopted Agile framework), so you can hit the ground running.

The Agile Manifesto

To make sense of Agile development practices, you must first understand the Agile philosophy. Agile was born in 2001 from collaboration between leaders in previous development processes such as Extreme Programming, Scrum, Feature-Driven Development, and Pragmatic Programming. The creators of the Agile process wrote the *Agile Manifesto* (*https://agilemanifesto.org/*) to describe the core tenets that undergird the process:

> *We are uncovering better ways of developing software by doing it and helping others do it. Through this work we have come to value:*
>
> **Individuals and interactions** *over processes and tools*
>
> **Working software** *over comprehensive documentation*
>
> **Customer collaboration** *over contract negotiation*
>
> **Responding to change** *over following a plan*
>
> *That is, while there is value in the items on the right, we value the items on the left more.*

The manifesto sounds a little quirky, but it gets at some important points. Agile practices focus on collaboration with teammates and customers; recognizing, accepting, and incorporating change; and focusing on iterative improvement over big-bang development releases. Agile is usually contrasted with *Waterfall*, an out-of-fashion practice where projects get exhaustively planned at their inception.

Ironically, once Agile became popular, black-belt ninjas, certifications, and process consultants overran some organizations. People got obsessed with the "right" way to "do Agile," often to the detriment of the very first principle: "individuals and interactions over processes and tools."

Agile Planning Frameworks

Scrum and Kanban are the two most common Agile planning frameworks. *Scrum*, the most popular, encourages short iterations with frequent checkpoints to adjust plans. Development work is broken into *sprints*. Sprint length varies, with two weeks being most common. At the beginning of a sprint, each team has a *sprint planning* meeting to divvy up work, which is captured in *user stories* or *tasks*. After planning, developers start on their work. Progress is tracked in a *ticketing* or *issue* system. A brief *stand-up* meeting takes place every day to share updates and call out problems. After each sprint, teams perform a *retrospective* to review finished work, discuss new findings, look at key metrics, and fine-tune the process. *Retrospectives (retros)* inform the next sprint's planning session, creating a feedback cycle from plan to development to retrospective and back to plan.

Kanban does not use fixed-length sprints like Scrum. Instead, Kanban defines workflow stages through which all work items transition (for example, backlog, planning, implementation, testing, deployment, rollout). Teams often customize Kanban stages to fit their needs. Kanban limits *work in progress (WIP)* by limiting the number of tasks in each stage. By limiting ticket count, teams are forced to finish existing tasks before taking on new work. Kanban boards are dashboards with vertical columns for each workflow stage. Tasks, represented by titled boxes, are moved between columns as status changes. Kanban boards visualize in-flight work and identify problems like piled-up work in a certain stage. If the board shows that a lot of work is stuck in the testing stage, for example, the team might make an adjustment by shifting some of the development work to a backlog, freeing up engineers to help with testing. Kanban works best for teams like support engineers and SREs that handle a large number of incoming requests rather than longer-term projects.

Teams rarely implement the "platonic ideal" of Scrum or Kanban; they pick and choose some practices and alter or ignore others. Whether your organization practices Scrum, Kanban, a mashup of the two called *Scrumban* (that's a real thing!), or some other variant of Agile, the planning process should be in service of delivering useful software to happy customers. Stay focused on the goals rather than the mechanics. Experiment and measure the results; keep what works and drop the rest.

Scrum

Most software teams practice some form of Scrum, so you'll need to understand how it works. All planning usually begins with prework. Developers and product managers create new *user stories*, and tickets from the *backlog* are *triaged*. Stories are assigned *story points* to estimate their complexity and are broken into *tasks*. Larger stories are designed and researched with *spike* stories. During *sprint planning*, the team chooses which stories to complete during the next sprint, using story points to prevent overcommitting.

User Stories

A user story is a specific kind of ticket that defines a feature request from a user's perspective, in the format "As a <user>, I <want to> <so that>." Here's an example: "As an administrator, I want to grant viewer permissions to my accountants so that they can see incoming billing statements." Writing user-centric descriptions keeps the focus on delivering user value.

A common misuse of user stories is to jam a regular task description into a story, as in "As a developer, I need to upgrade the shader plugin to version 8.7" or "As a user, I want the privacy policy to show up in the footer." A story like this misses the whole point. Why does the shader plugin need to be updated, what is the value this brings, and who wants it? Does a "user" want the policy, or does the compliance officer? If you are going to bother writing stories as opposed to tasks, write good ones.

Stories usually have attributes beside their title and description. The two most common are *estimates* and *acceptance criteria*. User story estimates are a guess at the effort a story takes to implement. Acceptance criteria define when a story is complete. Acceptance criteria keep developers, product managers, QA, and users on the same page. Try to write explicit tests for each acceptance criteria.

- The administrator permission page lists the "billing statements" option.

- Nonadministrator-granted "billing statements" viewer permission can see all of the account's billing statements.

- The Edit button is hidden on the billing statement page for non-administrator accounts.

- Nonadministrators with viewer permission are unable to edit billing statements.

- Nonadministrators with editor and viewer billing statement permissions are able to both see and edit billing statements.

Small stories often double as work tickets, while larger stories are linked to implementation tickets or subtasks. Stories that are ambiguous or need design are spiked. A spike is a time-bounded investigation that enables other stories to be completed. Spikes deliver a design doc, a build-versus-buy decision, an assessment of trade-offs, and so on. See Chapter 10 for more on design.

Tasks

A single story may need to be broken down into smaller tasks to estimate how long it will take, to share the work between multiple developers, and to track implementation progress. A good trick for breaking down work is to write very detailed descriptions. Read over the description and find all of the tasks.

We need to add a retry parameter to postProfile. Right now, profiles don't update if a network timeout occurs. We'll probably want to cap the retries and add exponential backoff so we don't block for too long; need to talk with product to find out how long they're willing to wait for a profile post to complete.

Once implemented, we should do both unit and integration tests. We should simulate real network timeouts in the integration tests to verify backoff is working correctly.

After testing, we need to deploy to our testing environment, then pro-
duction. In production, we should probably split the traffic and ramp
the retry behavior slowly, since `postProfile` *is pretty sensitive.*

Something as simple as adding a `retry` parameter to a network post actually has many steps: solidifying the specification with product managers, coding, unit testing, integration testing, deploying, and ramping. Breaking this work into subtasks helps track and coordinate all the steps.

Story Points

The team's work capacity is measured in *story points*, an agreed-upon sizing unit (measured in hours, days, or "complexity"). A sprint's capacity is the number of developers multiplied by the story points per developer; for example, a team with 4 engineers and 10 points per engineer would have a 40-point capacity. User-story time estimates are also defined in story points; the sum of all story points in a sprint should not be greater than a sprint's capacity.

Many teams use time-based allocations where a single point amounts to one workday. Day-based estimates usually account for nontask work—meetings, interruptions, code reviews, and so on—by defining a workday as four hours long.

Others define story points by task complexity, using a T-shirt size approach: one point is extra small, two points is small, three points is medium, five points is large, and eight points is extra large. Recognize the pattern? It's the Fibonacci sequence! Incrementing story points according to the Fibonacci sequence helps remove some of the quibbling about 3 versus 3.5 points. Having some gaps between point values also forces teams to make harder decisions about whether an item is big or small, not mediumish. The increase in the size of gaps for more complex tasks accounts for estimation inaccuracy in larger work.

Agile framework doctrine frowns upon time-based estimations. Practitioners claim that dates have emotional attachment and don't represent complexity. Nontime units can make it easier to express uncertainty. Changing a single method might seem like a small amount of work, but if that method is incredibly complex, it might require a lot of effort. It's mentally easier to say "This is a medium-complexity task" than "This will take me three full days of work."

People get very passionate about using time versus complexity for points, as well as their overall usefulness. We haven't found arguments on this topic to be very productive and recommend adopting whatever is most effective for your team.

Estimating story points is subjective; people tend to be poor estimators. One way to improve estimation accuracy is to use *relative sizing* to derive the values. Relative sizing is done by defining story points for tasks that have already been finished and then comparing the finished task to one that hasn't yet been worked on. If the unfinished task is less work, then it's probably fewer points; more work is probably more points; and if the tasks are similar, then they should be assigned the same value. Processes like *planning poker* are sometimes used, but even if you don't take part in them, looking at finished work will give you a feel for your team's story point values.

Backlog Triage

Backlog triage or *grooming* (in the tree-trimming sense) usually takes place before planning meetings. The backlog is a list of candidate stories. Triage is used to keep it fresh, relevant, and prioritized. Product managers read over the backlog with the engineering manager and sometimes with the developers. New stories are added, outdated stories are closed, incomplete stories are updated, and high-priority work is moved to the top of the backlog. A well-groomed backlog will drive planning meeting discussions.

Sprint Planning

A sprint planning meeting is held once prework is done. Planning meetings are collaborative; engineering teams work with product managers to decide what to work on. Prioritized stories are discussed, and engineers work with product managers to determine what will fit into the sprint's capacity.

Sprint capacity is determined by looking at how much was completed in previous sprints. Each sprint capacity is further refined during sprint planning as team members join or leave, go on vacation, or enter or exit on-call rotations.

The most important feature of a sprint is that it's short—usually two weeks. Short sprints make pushing out work doable since the work need only be pushed out at most a week or two. Small sprints force teams to break down large tasks into smaller ones. Small tasks are better because they're easier to understand and estimate. Breaking work into small tasks also allows more than one developer to work on a project simultaneously. Smaller development cycles with frequent touch points—stand-ups and reviews—mean problems surface earlier.

Sprints are considered locked once sprint planning is done. New work that surfaces during the sprint should not be pulled in; it should be pushed to the backlog and planned for a future sprint. Locking sprints lets developers focus on their work and brings predictability. When unplanned work does get pulled in, the team is expected to look into the reasons during the retrospective, with an eye to reducing unplanned work in the future.

Strict adherence to sprint planning practices is uncommon. Most teams pick and choose what they do; some do prework in the sprint planning meeting, and others have no product managers—developers define all work. Many teams don't use user stories, opting instead for task or bug tickets with more open-ended formats. Expect variation from team to team.

Stand-ups

After sprint planning is complete, work begins, and the team holds *stand-up meetings*, also called *scrum meetings* or *huddles*. Stand-ups keep everyone apprised of your progress, keep you accountable and focused, and give the team an opportunity to react to anything that puts sprint goals in danger.

Stand-ups are usually 15-minute meetings scheduled every morning (quick enough to stand through, though actual standing is optional). In the meeting format, teammates go around a circle and give an update on what they have worked on since the last stand-up, what they plan to work on going forward, and whether they've found any issues that can delay or derail the sprint. Though in-person stand-ups are the most common, some teams adopt an asynchronous format. In an asynchronous stand-up, the same update is submitted to a chatbot or group email on a daily cadence.

Stand-ups are a regular system check—the glance at your car's dashboard to ensure that you have gas and that its mysterious "check engine" light is not on. Updates should be fast; they are not a place for troubleshooting. Try to limit your comments on progress to just the bare essentials and raise any issues that you have. Announce discoveries, too; bugs that you discovered, unexpected behavior you found, and so on. Discussion about your discoveries can then happen in the *parking lot* (not the literal parking lot, of course).

If your team holds synchronous stand-ups, do your best to be on time. If your stand-ups involve updating the status on tickets or issues, try your best to update tickets assigned to you beforehand. When reading or listening to others' updates, you're looking for opportunities to help de-risk sprint completion: if someone says that a ticket is taking longer than expected, volunteer to help if you have spare time.

Parking lot discussions happen after the meeting. It's a way to keep the stand-ups brief and make sure that the discussions are relevant to everyone attending. When someone says to "save it for the parking lot," they're saying to stop the discussion and pick it up after the stand-up with interested parties.

Skipping the meeting when scheduling conflicts arise is acceptable. Ask your manager how to provide and get updates if you need to miss a stand-up. Asynchronous stand-ups are skipped less often.

There are many variations of stand-ups and scrums. You might catch phrases like *scrum of scrums* or *Scrumban*. Scrum of scrums is a model where a leader from each individual scrum meeting is selected to go to a second scrum where all the teams get together to report on their team progress and call out interdependencies between each other. Scrum of scrums are common in operations, where each team sends an engineer (usually the on-call) to an operations scrum to keep apprised of operational issues. Scrumban is an amalgamation of Scrum and Kanban. The important thing with all of this is to understand how your team and organization work, and to work within that framework.

Reviews

A review happens between each sprint. Reviews are usually broken into two parts: demonstrations and project review. During demonstrations, everyone on the team shows the progress they've made in the sprint. Afterward, the current sprint is evaluated against its goal. Successful sprints will meet their goals and have a high story-completion rate.

Review meeting structures vary widely. For some teams, demonstrations are the emphasis of the meeting, while other teams focus only on project status reviews. Many teams don't even have reviews. If your team has review meetings, take them seriously; provide real feedback and take pride in the work you've done. The value you get from reviews matches the effort you put into them.

It's standard to keep reviews to no more than one hour per sprint week—a two-week sprint would have a two-hour sprint review. Everyone gathers around desks or in a conference room for demonstrations. Teammates take turns showing what they've worked on. The meeting is kept informal. Afterward, sprint goals are reviewed and evaluated for completion.

Don't overprepare for sprint reviews. Spend a few minutes figuring out what you're going to show, and make sure your ticket statuses are accurate. Demonstrations are informal, so avoid formal presentations or speeches.

Reviews celebrate team wins, create unity, give feedback opportunities, and keep teams honest about progress. Not all developers in a team work on the same set of projects, so reviews help teammates keep up with what others are doing. Keeping teammates in sync gives everyone the opportunity to give feedback and to recognize great work; it creates cohesion. Project status reviews also help teams agree on what is truly "done" and how they are progressing toward their goals. Issues that are discovered can be discussed in sprint retrospectives.

Retrospectives

One of the 12 principles in the Agile Manifesto says, "At regular intervals, the team reflects on how to become more effective, then tunes and adjusts its behavior accordingly." Retrospective meetings address this principle.

In a retrospective, a team gets together to talk about what has and hasn't gone well since the last retrospective. The meeting normally has three phases: sharing, prioritization, and problem solving.

The leader (or *scrum master*) will kick off a retrospective by asking everyone to share what worked and what didn't during the last sprint. Everyone participates, and the scrum master keeps a list on the whiteboard or in a shared document. Teammates then discuss the priority of the items that haven't worked well—which are causing the most pain? Finally, the team brainstorms ways to address the highest priority problems.

Don't be afraid to change things. Agile development practices are meant to be malleable; it's in the manifesto: "Individuals and interactions over process and tools." Spend a few minutes before each retrospective to think about what would make your team better. Share your thoughts at the meeting.

Retrospectives and reviews often get confused. Reviews are focused on the work done in a sprint, while retrospectives focus on process and tooling. Retrospectives normally take place between sprints, often right after review meetings. Many teams combine a review, a retrospective, and a sprint planning meeting into a single meeting at the beginning of each sprint. A combined meeting is fine as long as each step—review, retro, and planning—is discretely addressed.

Retrospectives are also one of the reasons Agile comes in so many flavors. Teams are encouraged to reevaluate and adjust their processes frequently. Constant adjustment means no two teams practice Agile quite the same way.

Roadmaps

Two-week sprints are a good way to get small- and medium-sized work done, but larger projects need more advanced planning. Customers have delivery dates that developers need to stick to, the business needs to know which teams need more engineers, and large technical projects need to be broken down, planned, and coordinated.

Managers use product roadmaps for long-term planning. Roadmaps are typically broken into quarters: January through March, April through June, July through September, and October through December.

Planning takes place before each quarter begins. Engineering managers, product managers, engineers, and other stakeholders all convene to discuss upcoming goals and work. Planning usually involves a series of meetings and multiple rounds of discussion.

According to *The Papers of Dwight David Eisenhower*, Volume XI, Eisenhower said, "In preparing for battle I have always found that plans are useless, but planning is indispensable" (Johns Hopkins University Press, 1984). This applies to roadmaps. We've never seen a yearly or even quarterly roadmap be 100 percent accurate; this isn't the point. Roadmaps should encourage everyone to think long-term about what the team is building; they're not meant to be static and reliable documents about what the team will build nine months later. Quarters that are farther away should be fuzzier, while quarters that are closer should be more accurate. Don't fool yourself into thinking any quarter is 100 percent accurate.

Unlike sprints, which are locked, roadmaps are meant to evolve. Customer requirements will change, and new technical problems will arise. This is where sprint planning, reviews, and retrospectives help; they let you adjust your plan based on new information. Communication is critical when changing roadmaps. Dependent teams should be notified early that work is getting shuffled or dropped.

Many companies go through yearly planning cycles. Managers spend the last quarter of each year trying to plan the next four quarters of work for the upcoming year. Yearly planning is mostly theater—horse-trading and negotiating. Nonetheless, yearly planning cycles often drive "resource allocation" or "head count numbers"—corporate speak for where newly hired engineers end up. Annual planning usually focuses on large projects that account for a significant percentage of a team's time. Don't stress out if a project you are excited about isn't mentioned; ask your manager where the project stands at the end of the planning process.

Do's and Don'ts

DO'S	DON'TS
DO keep standup updates short.	**DON'T** obsess over the "right way" to do Agile.
DO write detailed acceptance criteria for stories.	**DON'T** be afraid to change Agile processes.
DO only commit to work in a sprint that you can actually finish.	**DON'T** force regular task descriptions into "stories."
DO break up large chunks of work if you can't finish them in a sprint.	**DON'T** forget to track planning and design work.

(continued)

DO'S	DON'TS
DO use story points to estimate work.	**DON'T** add work after sprints begin if committed work is not yet done.
DO use relative sizing and T-shirt sizing to help with estimation.	**DON'T** follow processes blindly.

Level Up

Most Agile books are going to be overkill for you. The books are extremely detailed and cover a lot of Agile variants; they're targeted at project and program managers. Stick to online resources.

The Agile Manifesto, which we mention in this chapter, has an additional page called "Principles Behind the Agile Manifesto" (*http:// agilemanifesto.org/principles.html*). Take a look at the principles for more details on the philosophy.

Atlassian's articles (*https://www.atlassian.com/agile/*) are a good source of practical information. You'll find articles on everything from project management and roadmap planning to DevOps in Agile. If your team uses Kanban rather than Scrum, Atlassian's Kanban article will be invaluable.

WORKING WITH MANAGERS

Building a working relationship with your manager will help you grow your career, reduce stress, and even ship reliable software. Working with your manager requires mutual understanding. You must understand what your manager needs so you can help them. Likewise, your manager must understand your needs so they can help you.

This chapter will help you build an effective relationship with your manager. We'll give you a short overview of the management profession: what your manager does and how they do it. We'll then discuss common management processes. Engineers often encounter abbreviations like 1:1s, PPPs, and OKRs, as well as terms like performance reviews, without knowing what they are, why they exist, or how they work. We'll give you a primer and show you how to get the most from them. We'll finish with tips to "manage up" and with a section on handling bad managers. By the end, you'll have a toolkit to build a productive relationship.

What Managers Do

Managers always seem to be in meetings, but it's not obvious what they are actually *doing*. Engineering managers work on people, product, and process. Managers build teams, coach and grow engineers, and manage interpersonal dynamics. Engineering managers also plan and coordinate product development. They might also weigh in on technical aspects of product development—code reviews and architecture—but good engineering managers rarely write code. Finally, managers iterate on team processes to keep them effective. Managers "manage" all of this by working with higher-level executives or directors ("up"), with other managers ("sideways"), and with their team ("down").

Managers manage up through relationships and communication with higher-level executives. Managers are the conduit between rank-and-file engineers and the executives making business decisions at the top. Upward management is crucial for getting resources (money and engineers) and making sure your team is recognized, appreciated, and heard.

Managers manage sideways by working with other managers. A manager has two teams: the collection of individuals they manage and their peer managers. This pool of peer managers works together to keep teams aligned on shared goals. Relationship maintenance, clear communication, and collaborative planning ensure that teams work together effectively.

Managers manage down by tracking the progress of ongoing projects; setting expectations and giving feedback; providing visibility into relative priorities; hiring and, if necessary, firing; and maintaining team morale.

Communication, Goals, and Growth Processes

Managers create processes to keep teams and individuals running smoothly. We covered the most common team-focused process framework, Agile, in Chapter 12. This section introduces you to processes you'll use to maintain your relationship with your manager.

One-on-ones (1:1s) and progress-plans-problems (PPP) reports are used for communication and updates, while objectives and key results (OKRs) and performance reviews manage goals and growth. These processes are most useful when you know what they are and how to use them.

1:1s

Your manager should schedule a weekly or biweekly 1:1 meeting with you. *One-on-ones* are a dedicated time for you and your manager to discuss critical topics, address big-picture concerns, and build a productive long-term relationship. One-on-ones are a well-known practice, but they're often run poorly as status check-ins or troubleshooting sessions.

You should set the agenda and do a lot of the talking in 1:1s. Prior to the meeting, share a bullet-point agenda with your manager. Keep a 1:1 document that contains past agendas and notes. Share your document with your manager and update it before and after each 1:1. Your manager can add their own items if they have topics to discuss, but your manager's agenda should take a back seat to yours.

We hit on two important points, so we're going to stop and restate them: you set the agenda in a 1:1, and 1:1s are not for status updates. These two points alone can make the difference between hours and hours of wasted time and very productive and important conversations. Use the following prompts as topics for discussion:

BIG PICTURE　What questions do you have about the company's direction? What questions do you have about organizational changes?

FEEDBACK　What could we be doing better? What do you think of the team's planning process? What is your biggest technical concern? What do you wish you could do that you can't? What is your biggest problem? What is the company's biggest problem? What roadblocks are you or others on the team encountering?

CAREER   What career advice does your manager have for you? What can you improve on? What skills do you wish you had? What are your long-term goals, and how do you feel you're tracking in them?

PERSONAL   What's new in your life? What personal issues should your manager be aware of?

One-on-ones create mutual understanding and connection. It's normal to talk a bit about seemingly irrelevant topics—your cat, your manager's love of colorful sneakers, the weather. You are working on building a relationship that's deeper than an exchange of code for salary. Personal and off-topic conversations are important, but don't let every 1:1 become a social visit.

If you haven't received a 1:1 invitation, ask if your manager conducts them. Not all do, but it's common. If your manager doesn't do 1:1s, ask them how they prefer for you to discuss typical 1:1 topics. Some managers prefer "lazy" 1:1s; they leave it up to individuals to set up a time to talk. If no meeting is scheduled, managers assume there's nothing to discuss. You should have something to talk about most weeks; that's a long list we just gave you.

If your manager repeatedly cancels your 1:1s, you need to speak to them about it. Part of their job is to manage their team, and part of management is investing time with you. Being "too busy" is not an excuse. If they can't find time to conduct a 1:1 with you, the issue should be addressed. Calling out repeated 1:1 cancellations can be a valuable signal for a manager. Such a conversation need not (should not!) be a confrontation; it's the type of feedback your manager wants and needs.

THE LOST 1:1

Dmitriy was once part of a reorganization that jumbled teams around. He ended up with almost 20 direct reports, some of whom he'd been friendly with for many years, while others were new. There was a lot to do—get to know the new folks, establish a roadmap for the team, improve old systems, and create new ones. A full year later, Dmitriy discovered that since they were on friendly terms, Dmitriy had forgotten to establish a regular check-in with one of his reports! He didn't make the discovery until the employee set up time to say that they wanted to switch to another team—and one of the reasons was that they wanted a manager who would be more involved in their career development. An existing friendly relationship is not a substitute. A manager who is too busy to do 1:1s might be too busy to be a manager!

You can set up 1:1s with people other than your manager, too. Reach out to those who you think you could learn from. In fact, 1:1s with senior engineers are particularly helpful if your company does not have a formal mentoring program; 1:1s are also a good way to get familiar with different parts of the organization. Again, make sure you have an agenda so you don't fall back on "status check-in" 1:1s.

PPPs

A *PPP* is a commonly used status update format. A status update isn't meant to account for your time; it's meant to help your manager find problems, areas where you need context, and opportunities to connect you with the right people. Updates also surface topics for 1:1 discussion and help you reflect on where you've been, where you're going, and what stands in the way.

As the name implies, PPPs have a section for each of the P's (progress, plans, and problems). Each section should have three to five bullet points in it, and each bullet point should be short, just one to three sentences. Here's an example:

2022-07-02

PROGRESS

- Debugged performance issue with notification service
- Code review up for email templating in notification service
- Spam detection service design circulated and milestone 0 service written

PLANS

- Add metrics and monitoring to spam detection service
- Work with tools team to support PyPI artifacts in secure build environment
- Help onboard new hire—doing a code walk-through of spam detection service
- Work with database administrator to add index to preemptively fix performance issue on notification service before load increases for the holiday

PROBLEMS

- Having trouble getting team to code review my PRs—several pending
- Redis stability is an issue
- Interview load feels high—averaging four per week

Share PPPs with your manager and anyone else who is interested—usually via email, Slack, or a wiki. Updates happen periodically, usually weekly or monthly, depending on the organization.

PPP updates are easy if you keep a log of past PPPs. Every time a new PPP is due, create a new entry. Look at your problems from the last PPP and ask yourself, have any problems been solved? Are any problems persisting? Solved problems go in the progress section of the new PPP. Persisting problems stay in the problems section. Next, look at your plans section from the previous PPP: Have you finished any of your planned work? If so, add it to the progress section of the new PPP. If not, are you planning on working on the task before the next PPP, or was there a problem that impeded progress on your planned work? Update the plans or problems section accordingly. Finally, look at your upcoming work and calendar. Update the plans section with any new work you are expecting to do before the next PPP is due. The whole process should take less than five minutes.

OKRs

The *OKR framework* is a way for companies to define goals and measure their success. In the OKR framework, companies, teams, and individuals all define goals (objectives) and attach metrics (key results) to each objective. Each objective has three to five key results, which are metrics that signal progress toward the objective.

An engineer working on stabilizing an order service might define their OKRs like this:

OBJECTIVE Stabilize order service

KEY RESULT 99.99 percent uptime as measured by health check

KEY RESULT 99th-percentile latency (P99) < 20 ms

KEY RESULT 5XX error rate below 0.01 percent of responses

KEY RESULT Support team can execute regional failover in less than five minutes

Ideally, OKRs flow from the top of the company, through teams, all the way to each individual. Each individual's OKRs contribute to the goals of their team, and each team's OKRs contribute to the goals of the company. The engineer's OKR, shown previously, might feed into a team OKR to improve stability, which might feed into a company OKR to improve customer satisfaction.

Don't make the key results a to-do list. They should spell out not how to *do* something but rather how you'll *know* when something is done. There are many ways to reach an objective, and your OKRs should not box you into a particular plan. A silly example sometimes helps illustrate this point better: if your objective is to make it to Grandma's birthday party, the key result is "be in Los Angeles by the 20th," not "drive down I-5 on the 19th." Taking the scenic route down the 1 or flying are perfectly acceptable alternative ways to make it to Los Angeles, and a well-formulated OKR gives us freedom to choose the right method at the time we need to make that choice, not when we set the OKR.

Objectives and key results are usually defined and evaluated quarterly. Work with your manager to understand company and team objectives. Use the higher-level objectives to define your OKRs. Try to have as few OKRs as possible; it'll keep you focused. Between one and three OKRs per quarter is a sweet spot. More than five and you're spreading yourself too thin.

OKRs are commonly set slightly higher than reasonable to create "reach" or "stretch" goals. This philosophy implies that you should not complete 100 percent of your reach-goal OKRs; this is a sign that you aren't shooting high enough. Most OKR implementations shoot for a 60 percent to 80 percent success rate, meaning 60 to 80 percent of the objectives are met. If you're hitting more than 80 percent of your objectives, you're not being ambitious; below 60 percent and you're not being realistic or are failing to meet expectations. (Why not set the OKRs at 100 percent and reward overachieving? Multiple ambitious goals give you flexibility on what to drop midquarter and don't require the precision that a 100 percent completion expectation would.) Make sure you understand whether your company treats OKRs as must-have goals or ambitious targets with some expected failure rate!

Some companies use qualitative goals instead of OKRs. Others drop the "O" and focus only on the metrics—*key performance indicators (KPIs)*—without stating the objective explicitly. Regardless of the framework, individuals and teams need a way to set goals and evaluate progress. Make sure you know what your goals are and how success is evaluated.

Not all companies set individual goals; some set only team-, department-, or company-level OKRs. If your company does this, it's still a good idea to explicitly talk with your manager about expectations and how they're measured.

Performance Reviews

Managers conduct formal performance reviews at a regular cadence, usually annually or semiannually. Title and compensation adjustments are generally made during review time, too. Reviews are conducted using a tool or template with prompts like this:

- What have you done this year?

- What went well this year?

- What could have gone better this year?

- What do you want in your career? Where do you see yourself in three to five years?

Employees self-evaluate first, and then managers respond. Finally, the manager and employee get together to discuss feedback. Employees normally need to sign off on the evaluation document after the discussion to acknowledge receiving it.

Don't work off memory when writing your self-review. Memory is spotty, and you might fixate on only certain memorable projects. Keep an up-to-date list of the work you completed throughout the year—a completed to-do list, a set of PPPs, or a bullet journal—to jog your memory. Look at the tasks you completed in your company's issue tracker. What milestones, epics, and stories did you work on? Merged pull requests and code reviews also show work you've done. Don't forget your nonengineering projects. Mentoring interns, code reviews, conducting interviews, blog posts, presentations, documentation—all of this should be recognized. Use what you have to write an honest self-review.

Performance reviews can be stressful. Try to see a review as an opportunity to look back at what you've accomplished and to talk about what you want to do next; to openly acknowledge missed opportunities; to develop a growth plan for the next year; and to give feedback to your manager. You should never be surprised by your performance review feedback; if you are, talk with your manager about the communication breakdown. A successful performance review should give you concrete actions to achieve your goals.

You might also be asked to participate in *360s* (as in "360 degrees"), where employees solicit feedback from coworkers in all directions: above (managers), below (reports), and sideways (peers). Coworkers answer questions like "What could I be doing better?" and "What are people afraid to tell me?" and "What am I doing well?" Ultimately, 360s encourage honest feedback and give employees an opportunity to tell managers how they're doing. Take 360s seriously and give thoughtful notes.

Managers should be giving feedback frequently throughout the year—during 1:1s, as an aside after a meeting, or over chat. If you're not getting enough feedback, ask your manager how you're doing in your next 1:1. You can also ask mentors or senior engineers.

Managing Up

Just as managers manage up to higher-level executives and directors, you "manage up" by helping your manager and making sure they help you. You can help your manager by giving them feedback. They can help you by giving you feedback and helping you achieve your goals. And don't settle if things aren't working out. Dysfunctional management can be traumatic and damage your growth.

Get Feedback

Reviews and 360s provide holistic feedback, but they are too infrequent to be relied upon solely. You need regular feedback so you can adjust quickly. Managers don't always volunteer feedback, so you might have to ask.

Use 1:1s to get feedback. Send questions to your manager beforehand; giving extemporaneous feedback is hard. Ask for specific feedback. "What can I do to get better with testing?" is better than "What can I do better?" Don't limit feedback requests to technical questions. Ask for feedback on communication, career growth, leadership, learning opportunities, and so on. Use the prompts in the previous 1:1 section if you need ideas.

Don't take feedback at face value. Your manager is just one perspective (albeit an important one). Try to incorporate your manager's feedback into your perspective rather than adopting your manager's feedback outright. Ask yourself what gaps your manager has in their perspective, how their feedback fits with yours, what they know that you don't, and so on.

Give feedback on feedback, too. It can feel like feedback goes into a black hole. Tell your manager when their feedback pays off: "I joined the engineering reading group, like you suggested, and it's been really fun to read papers and discuss them with engineers from other teams! Thanks so much for the idea. I'm learning a ton." Positive results will encourage them to give more feedback. And let your manager know if feedback isn't working out; they might have other ideas: "I joined the engineering reading group, like you suggested, and to be honest, it's not working for me. They are discussing papers that aren't super relevant to my work. Can you suggest other ways for me to develop connections to different teams?"

You can also give feedback by asking for feedback. Asking how to do something will often expose gaps in processes. The answer to "How could

I have prevented the production incident last week?" might be "We need to build a test environment." Give your manager the opportunity to reach a conclusion by asking for feedback rather than proposing a solution.

Give Feedback

Good managers want feedback from their team. Managers need to know how things are going—what's working and what's not. Every individual on the team is going to have a unique perspective. Feedback eliminates blind spots.

Feedback can be about anything: the team, the company, behavior, projects, technical plans, or even human resource policies. Raise problems, but don't focus solely on them. Positive feedback is just as valuable: it can be hard for managers to know which changes had a positive effect, and their work doesn't have unit tests.

Use the *Situation-Behavior-Impact (SBI) framework* when providing feedback. First describe the *situation*. Then, describe the *behavior*: a specific behavior you find praiseworthy or problematic. Finally, explain the *impact*: the effect of the behavior and the reason it's important. Here is an example:

Situation: *I finished up all the code changes to the new permissions service in January and handed it off to the operations team for roll-out, but the service is still not deployed as of today, at the beginning of March.*

Behavior: *The "upcoming releases" dashboard has moved the expected release date every week for the past five weeks. The database upgrade has also been pending for several weeks.*

Impact: *This means we're in danger of missing our deadlines, and a number of dependent projects are also delayed. Is there anything we can do?*

The SBI framework avoids character judgments and assumptions about intention and motivation. Instead, it focuses on the facts and observable impact and steers the discussion toward mitigation and prevention.

Note that you do not recommend a solution in the SBI framework. You might have solutions in mind, but it's best to start with the issue and learn more before making recommendations. You might discover that you were missing valuable information or that a problem looks different than you thought. Discuss your solution ideas at the end of the conversation, after you've had the chance to consider the problem from a different perspective.

Give feedback privately, calmly, and frequently. One-on-ones are an excellent venue. Feedback can trigger strong emotions, but try to maintain a clear head and keep the conversation constructive. Giving feedback in private permits your manager to have an honest conversation with you and can keep both parties from feeling attacked. Frequent feedback eliminates surprises. Don't wait for a problem to fester until it's too late.

It doesn't have to be all doom and gloom. The SBI framework works for positive feedback, too:

Situation: *We needed to write a design doc for proposed changes to the sign-up workflow last week and I took the opportunity to use the new design doc template you created.*

Behavior: *The section on rollout and communication plans made us realize we completely forgot to loop the user support team in on the changes.*

Impact: *They gave us a bunch of helpful feedback once we reached out! And it was much faster to write the document because we didn't need to think about how it should be structured. Thanks for working on this!*

Whether it's feedback to your manager or your peers, and whether it's written or verbal, always try to make it the kind of feedback you would want to receive. Ask yourself, what problem are you trying to solve? What is the outcome you wish for—what does success look like?

Discuss Your Goals

Don't expect your manager to know what you want from your career. You need to clearly articulate your goals and aspirations for your manager to help you achieve them. Formal reviews are a great place for such conversations.

If you don't have career goals yet, that's fine. Tell your manager you want to explore; they'll be able to help. If you have interests beyond your immediate focus, let them know. Don't limit yourself to engineering, either. You might find product management fascinating or have the ambition to start a company. Think big and long-term. For example, you might say:

> *Can we talk about career paths today? I'm honestly not sure where I see myself in five years or what my options even are. What are some of the common career paths you see and how do they differ? I'm enjoying my current project, but I am also curious about security. Are there opportunities coming up that might let me do something security-related?*

If you know what you want to do, let your manager know and work with them to steer your work toward your destination. Part of a manager's job is to align your interests with the needs of the company; the more they know about your interests, the more they can steer the right opportunities your way.

Be patient after discussing your goals. There are only so many opportunities available. It's ultimately up to you to make the most of what you're given. Recognize that opportunities come in many forms: new projects, new challenges, interns to mentor, presentation opportunities, blog posts to write, training, or teams to partner with. Under the right lens, everything you do is an opportunity for growth.

ESTABLISH YOUR SUPPORT NETWORK

It can be difficult to give feedback, to deal with certain situations, or even to know what is normal and what is not. Trusted peer groups, both within and outside your organization, are a good way to sanity-check things. This goes double for members of underrepresented groups. Seek out organizations like PyLadies, /dev/color, and other communities who can talk through your situation and share their stories and experiences.

Take Action When Things Aren't Working

Every employee/manager relationship is unique, so it's difficult to give general advice. Each situation depends on the company, the team, the manager, and the employee. All we can say for certain is that you should be proactive if you feel things aren't working.

Relationships and jobs have ups and downs. A short-term rough patch can happen and doesn't need drastic action. If, however, you are feeling consistent frustration, stress, or unhappiness, you should speak up.

Use the SBI framework (from the "Give Feedback" section) to talk to your manager if you feel comfortable doing so. Speak to human resources (HR), your manager's manager, or other mentors if you aren't comfortable speaking to your manager. The course you pursue depends on your relationship with each party. If you have nowhere to turn, use HR.

HR's role is to maintain stability and keep the company out of legal and compliance trouble, which is not quite the same as making things right or fair. If nothing else, talking to HR ensures that there is a record of your concern. Companies do tend to react to *patterns* of concerns.

If you're told things will change, give your manager time—three to six months is reasonable. Managers need to think about feedback and implement changes. Processes or even organizational structures might have to be rebuilt. Opportunities to demonstrate change might be infrequent. Pay attention to the "slope" of change: Are things improving? Have you seen a commitment to improvement demonstrated through concrete actions?

If time passes and you are still unhappy, it might be time for a transfer to another internal team or a new job. Internal transfers work well when you like your coworkers and company. A new company is better when problems are more systemic: a bad business, poor leadership, a toxic culture. Switching teams can be delicate; talk with the manager you want to transfer to and then with your current manager. Expect a team transition to take time as you hand off work to others, but don't allow team changes to take longer than three months.

THE PROGRAMMER IN THE MIRROR

Dmitriy's first job as a software engineer almost caused him to drop out of tech altogether. His tech lead for several years was a well-meaning person, a very good programmer, friendly, and, in retrospect, an absolutely terrible manager. He regularly made comments like "I thought UC Berkeley [Dmitriy's alma mater] was supposed to be a good school" and "A real programmer would instead . . . ," and he made jokes about firing people. He even installed a bicycle mirror on his monitor to watch Dmitriy's screen. Here's the kicker: he had good reason to resort to a mirror. After a few years in this environment, Dmitriy had become completely unmotivated, didn't have faith in his own abilities, and was slacking off a lot. He gave serious consideration to ditching it all and becoming a chiropractor.

After some soul-searching, Dmitriy decided to give it another try at a different company. His next gig turned out to be the direct opposite, culture-wise. His new teammates had low ego, a lot of skill, and were convinced Dmitriy could solve any problem they threw at him given the right support. Dmitriy's confidence grew and, with it, his motivation, focus, and skills. His career rebounded; it all worked out. But it almost didn't happen because of one very good programmer who was a very bad manager.

Dysfunctional management is frustrating, stressful, and can stunt your career growth. Not every manager is good, and not every good manager is a good fit for you. If you've given feedback and been patient but things still aren't working, move on.

Do's and Don'ts

DO'S	DON'TS
DO expect managers to be accessible and transparent.	**DON'T** hide difficulties from your manager.
DO tell your manager what you need.	**DON'T** use 1:1s as a status update meeting.
DO set the agenda for your 1:1s.	**DON'T** work from memory when writing self-reviews.
DO keep 1:1 notes.	**DON'T** write superficial feedback.
DO write actionable feedback of the sort you'd like to receive.	**DON'T** get boxed in by OKRs.
DO track accomplishments to make self-reviews easier.	**DON'T** take feedback as an attack.
DO use the SBI framework to make feedback less personal.	**DON'T** put up with bad management.
DO think about long-term career goals.	

Level Up

A good way to understand your manager is to read the books they read. Engineering management books will help you understand why your managers are doing what they're doing. It'll also build empathy; you'll be exposed to some of the problems they deal with. Plus, you'll pick up useful skills and be able to give better feedback to your manager.

Start by reading *The Manager's Path* by Camille Fournier (O'Reilly Media, 2017). Fournier's book walks you through the phases of a manager from a staff engineer through a VP of engineering. It discusses how each level of manager operates and gives more details on management processes like 1:1s. The book will also help you chart your own career path.

Will Larson's *An Elegant Puzzle* (Stripe Press, 2019) gives insight into the problems a manager faces and the frameworks they use to manage them.

Thanks for the Feedback by Douglas Stone and Sheila Heen (Penguin Books, 2014) will help you process review feedback. Feedback is an emotionally fraught topic. This book gives you tools to get the most out of feedback "even when it is off base, unfair, poorly delivered, and, frankly, you're not in the mood." Many of the book's tools work well in other types of conversations, too.

Managing Up by Mary Abbajay (Wiley, 2018) takes our "Managing Up" section to the next level. The book discusses manager personas and how to deal with them. It also gives solid advice on tough managers and discusses what to do when it's time to move on.

Andy Grove's book *High Output Management* (Vintage, 2015) is the classic book on engineering management. Written in 1983, Grove documents the philosophy and practices he cultivated at Intel—philosophies that have shaped modern engineering management. You should read it for historical context but also because it's still really relevant. Chances are your manager has read it, so you'll have a common reference point.

NAVIGATING YOUR CAREER

A software engineer's career arc is long. *The Missing README* will take you to the end of the beginning of your journey. What lies beyond is a lifetime of learning, technical leadership, and maybe even management or entrepreneurship. Regardless of your path, you must continue to grow.

While previous chapters focused on specific engineering activities, we'll zoom out in this chapter to look at what lies ahead, give career advice, and share some closing thoughts.

To Senior and Beyond

Career ladders list job title hierarchies and describe expectations at each level. Together, the titles in a ladder form a career progression at a company. The number of levels vary from company to company, but there are usually two transitions that indicate significant shifts in seniority: from junior or software engineer to senior engineer, and from senior to staff or principal engineer.

In Chapter 1, we enumerated the technical, execution, communication, and leadership skills expected of a senior engineer. Importantly, a senior engineer's scope and focus also change. Junior engineers implement features and complete tasks. Senior engineers deal with more uncertainty and ambiguity; they help determine what to work on, tackle larger or more critical projects, and need less direction.

Staff engineers take on even broader responsibilities that extend beyond their team. They contribute to engineering strategy, quarterly planning, system architecture, and run engineering processes and policies. Staff engineers still code (and they code a lot), but to get to this level, just being a good coder isn't enough: you have to understand the big picture and make decisions with far-reaching consequences.

Career ladders usually split into management and "individual contributor" tracks at the staff level. Advancing in your career does not *require* managing people, and management is a wholly different skillset. If you're considering management, read Camille Fournier's book *The Manager's Path* (O'Reilly Media, 2017) to get a glimpse of what's in store.

Career Advice

Becoming a senior or staff engineer takes time and persistence, but you can help yourself by taking responsibility for your career growth. Cultivate a T-shaped skillset, participate in engineering programs, engage in the promotion process, don't change jobs too frequently, and pace yourself.

Be T-Shaped

Software engineering has many specialties: frontend, backend, operations, data warehousing, machine learning, and so on. "T-shaped" engineers work effectively in most areas and are experts in at least one.

We first encountered the concept of T-shaped people in Valve's *Handbook for New Employees* (*https://www.valvesoftware.com/en/publications/*). The handbook describes T-shaped people as:

> *... people who are both generalists (highly skilled at a broad set of valuable things—the top of the T) and also experts (among the best in their field within a narrow discipline—the vertical leg of the T).*

Being a T-shaped engineer will keep you from making decisions in a vacuum, allow you to make changes that touch multiple codebases, and simplify troubleshooting. You'll be able to solve hard problems that stump others by combining your expertise with the ability to understand disparate systems.

Start by building your base. Base-building will expose you to different subfields so you can find your passion. Look for projects that involve other teams such as data science, operations, frontend, and so on. Work with other teams' code and ask if it's okay to contribute patches or pair program as changes are made. Delve deeper to acquire depth as you encounter subjects and problems that pique your interest.

Keep the breadth/depth paradigm in mind with your team, too. Everyone has their own expertise and gaps. Just because your teammate doesn't know what a monad is doesn't mean that they aren't good at something else. Likewise, don't be too hard on yourself if you find you're the novice in a conversation; you will have other areas of comparative strength.

A good team will have a solid mix of T-shaped people. Product development teams are likely to have varied areas of depth among teammates, while infrastructure teams are more likely to have a shared expertise.

As companies grow, they increasingly hire specialists for each area, which will push everyone that's already at the company to also specialize (since generalists will find themselves with a smaller and smaller area to operate). This process might drive you toward specialization or, if you already have a T-shaped skillset, help you gracefully adapt as you get to lean more on your specialty. You might even find that some of the specialists who join the company don't have your breadth (they're not T-shaped), so you can help them understand their surroundings and be more effective.

Participate in Engineering Programs

Many companies have engineering programs that encourage learning, development, and a shared culture. Hiring, interviewing, brown bags, conferences, meetups, reading groups, open source projects, and apprenticeship and mentoring programs are all opportunities to get involved.

Seek out and join the programs that most interest you. You can participate by attending or by leading. If you find your company doesn't have well-organized engineering programs, create one! Discuss your ideas with management and find passionate teammates that want to help.

Participating in and contributing to engineering programs will help your career. You'll build relationships, increase your visibility across the organization, learn new skills, and help influence company culture.

Steer Your Promotion

Ideally, your manager would promote you at the exact right and fair time. But the world is rarely ideal, so you'll probably need to steer your promotion. Learn the promotion process, make sure your work is valuable and visible, and speak up when you think you're nearing the next level.

To get promoted, you'll need to know how you're evaluated and what the promotion process looks like. Find your company's career ladder to determine the skills you need for the next level. Talk with your manager about the promotion process. Are promotions done annually? Who evaluates potential promotions? Do you need a mentor, sponsor, or promotion packet?

Once you understand the evaluation criteria and promotion process, do a self-assessment and get feedback from others. Write a brief document that lists your achievements for each category of the career ladder. Look for areas that you need to develop. Solicit feedback from your manager, peers, and mentors. Tell people why you are asking for feedback so they know you aren't just looking for reassurance. Dig into specifics:

- "If you compare my design docs to those by some Level 3 engineers, are there differences that are apparent?"

- "You said I write good tests. Which tests that I wrote do you find good? What's an example of less-good tests? Who at our company writes *great* tests? How is what I do different from what they do?"

If you get feedback you disagree with, try to understand where it's coming from. Others might have an incomplete view of your work, or your work might not be perceived as valuable. Perhaps team shuffling left you without a completed project to point to. Or maybe your evaluation of your own work is a bit off and you need to recalibrate. Address feedback misalignment with candid conversations with your manager.

After you self-assess and get feedback, review everything with your manager and work out a plan to fill in gaps. Expect suggestions about engineering programs to join or projects and practices that exercise certain skills.

People are often disappointed when they expect a promotion for the wrong reasons. A promising but unfinished project isn't enough; managers want to see results. Technical skills are necessary but not sufficient: you must work well with others, contribute to team goals, and help the organization. A promotion isn't a function of time: whether you are in your job for one year or five, impact is what matters. When you hit the next level, expect to be there for three to six months before promotion so you prove you can consistently meet the bar.

When it comes to promotion conversations, timing matters. Start these conversations *before* you think you are ready for a promotion— about when you've hit the halfway point. Engaging early gives you and your manager time to align and address gaps. If you wait until you already think you deserve a promotion, but your manager doesn't agree, the conversation becomes about resolving a conflict rather than coming up with a plan.

Finally, be aware that career ladders reflect common molds that not everyone fits into. Staff work requires broad influence and "glue work" (coordination, process improvements, documentation, communication, and so on). At the senior level and below, requirements are often described more in terms of pure coding ability. This creates a problem for junior engineers who take on essential noncoding work that does not have a Git commit attached to it. Such engineers spend less time coding, so their promotions get delayed, or they get pushed to a different role such as project management. Tanya Reilly's talk and blog post (*https:// noidea.dog/glue/*) suggests that you *stop doing glue work*—even if it hurts the team in the short term—if your manager does not see your contributions as a path to promotion. This is a tough pill to swallow, and it may seem unfair, but the onus for making things fair here is on management, not on you.

Change Jobs Carefully

Changing jobs can expand your skillset and your network, but frequent job changes can stunt your growth and look bad to hiring managers. Don't change jobs without a good reason.

Senior engineers leverage past experience to guide decisions. If you constantly switch jobs, you'll never see how your decisions play out over the long term, which will stunt the development of the intuition you need as a senior engineer. Hiring managers see a series of short stints on a résumé as a red flag: they worry that you will leave as soon as the going gets tough and the initial "honeymoon" period is over.

FOMO—fear of missing out—isn't a good reason to switch jobs. From the outside, other companies appear to have newer technology, cooler problems, and none of the complications of your current company. The grass will always look greener on the other side, but all companies have problems. If you are worried about missing out, expose yourself to new ideas at meetups and conferences. Employers will often pay for career development or even schooling. Open source and side projects are also a good way to stay fresh if your schedule allows it. You might also consider staying at the same company but switching teams.

There are, of course, good reasons to change jobs even after a short tenure. Some companies or teams are a bad fit, and it's better to get out of a bad situation quickly rather than letting it drag on. Exceptional opportunities don't arrive on a convenient schedule, and you should be open to them when they appear. There's also value in exposing yourself to different technology stacks, coworkers, and engineering organizations. And engineering salaries have been growing rapidly; your company might not be awarding raises as fast as the market is rising. Sadly, it is often easier to catch up to the market by switching jobs. But stick with your job if you're still properly compensated, growing, and learning. There is great value in seeing teams, companies, and software evolve over time.

Conversely, don't stay too long. Job ossification—becoming stagnant—is a legitimate reason to change things up. Longtime engineers at a company naturally become historians who educate engineers about how things work, who knows what, and why things were done the way they were. Such knowledge is valuable—it's even part of being a staff engineer—but it can stunt your growth if your value comes more from past work than current contributions. Changing companies and finding yourself in a new environment can kickstart your growth.

Pace Yourself

The software field isn't stress free. Work can be hectic, competition is fierce, technology evolves quickly, and there's always more to learn. It might feel like there's too much happening too fast. New engineers often react by pushing harder and working longer hours, but that's a recipe for burnout. Take breaks to disconnect, and don't overwork yourself.

Engineers sometimes glorify 14-hour workdays and sleeping bags under the desk, but marathon coding sessions and lack of sleep will damage your code, your health, and your relationships. Researchers studying the effect of sleep on developer performance found that "a single night of sleep deprivation leads to a reduction of 50% in the quality of the implementations" ("Need for Sleep: The Impact of a Night of Sleep Deprivation on Novice Developers' Performance," *IEEE Transactions on Software Engineering*, 2020). Yes, you'll occasionally have long hours, but don't let it become a habit or, worse, your identity. Long hours and poor sleep aren't sustainable; the debt comes due.

Even with a healthy work schedule, the monthly grind of work can burn you out. Take vacations and sabbaticals to disconnect. Some engineers prefer large vacations at the end of the year, while others take quarterly vacations to stave off fatigue. Find what works for you, but don't let vacation days go to waste. Most companies cap the maximum number of vacation days you can accrue. Some companies also offer sabbaticals, typically one-to-three-month extended breaks, to explore and refresh.

Your career is a marathon, not a sprint; you have decades ahead of you. Pace yourself and enjoy the journey!

Closing Thoughts

Software engineering is a great career filled with fascinating challenges. You can contribute to any industry, from science to farming, health, entertainment, or even space exploration. Your work can improve billions of lives. Work with people you like on problems you're passionate about, and you can accomplish great things. We're rooting for you. Good luck.

INDEX

The Missing README is set in Faustina Pro and Din Pro. The book was printed and bound by Sheridan Books, Inc. in Chelsea, Michigan.